The
SEASONAL
VEGAN

The
SEASONAL
VEGAN

Sarah Philpott

SEREN

SEREN

is the book imprint of
Poetry Wales Press Ltd.
57 Nolton Street, Bridgend, Wales, CF31 3AE

www.serenbooks.com
facebook.com/SerenBooks
twitter: @SerenBooks

© **Sarah Philpott, 2020**
Photographs © Manon Houston, 2020

ISBN 978-1-78172-587-0

A CIP record for this title is available
from the British Library.

The publisher works with the financial
assistance of the Books Council of Wales.

Cover photograph: © Manon Houston,
www.manonhouston.com

Printed in Glasgow
by Bell & Bain Ltd.

Contents

Introduction

The recipes

Introduction

'One cannot think well, love well, sleep well,
if one has not dined well.' – *Virginia Woolf*

My food diary

I think of my life as a series of meals. I don't remember my first bite of sweet summer strawberries, although I'm almost certain they sat in a pool of cream topped with a sprinkling of snowy sugar – or as a smear of pinky red jam atop a Sara Lee cheesecake.

For me, my most moreish memories consist of countless rounds of toast with Marmite, Mum's Sunday roasts, and big bowls of tomato soup. I remember one Pancake Day when I polished off so many pancakes that I was sick in the middle of the night. These culinary rites of passage remind me of where I come from, who I once was and who I am now.

I ate a lot as a kid (I still do) but until I reached the age of about eight or nine I had hollow legs. The puppy fat years followed and they continued well into my early twenties, but luckily for me, I've made my peace with eating. My food diaries used to count calories; now they see me through the seasons. When I wrote *The Occasional Vegan*, I wanted to show people how easy it is to eat in a balanced way as a vegan. There's no need to miss out on flavour and you can even knock a few pounds off the cost of your weekly shop. I want to dig into the abundance of seasonal produce that grows right here on our fair isle. Although vegans eat much more than rabbit food, we base our meals around fruits and vegetables so it makes sense to make them the stars of the show.

Now, I'm no gardener and I've never grown my own vegetables – not yet, anyway – and we don't have a garden in the flat where I live with Kieron, Seren and Bobbie the cat. I've always been a city dweller (I was born and bred in Cardiff, spent my university days in Leeds and now live in sometimes sunny Swansea) but I love nature and I notice the change in the air as every month goes by. When I go food shopping, my first stop is always the fruit and vegetable aisle, where I watch the colours change from red to orange then green and back again across the course of the year. Wouldn't it be dull if we ate the same all year round? Nothing beats a warm stew with squash when it's cold outside, and bright and beaming beetroot pop out from underground to guide us through the darker months. Spring bounds up to us with all things green, and when summer arrives we can enjoy succulent strawberries, rhubarb, Jersey Royal potatoes, asparagus, broad beans and peas.

Although I like to eat and cook with the seasons, I do it in a practical way – I shop like this purely because it tastes better, is often cheaper and because it's better for the environment. Eating seasonally is sometimes seen as inaccessible or elitist, but it isn't. As someone who usually does the weekly shop at the supermarket, I sometimes have to look a bit harder to see what's in season, but it's there all right. When I get the chance, I try the better greengrocers in Swansea and as a rare treat, I head to the local farmers' market in Cardiff or Swansea. I don't have time for food snobbery but I do like eating as well as I can on a budget. As a freelancer, part of my job involves chasing invoices and money doesn't exactly grow on trees, so I have to shop carefully.

Because I often work from home, cooking marks the end of the day, when I have to stop writing and prepare an evening meal, although as I live with a pair of fussy eaters, it's often just for me, unless we have friends over. As much as I love feeding others, cooking for myself is just as fun. The dishes in this book range from simple suppers to some that require a little more elbow grease but they all use ingredients that are easy to get hold of and can easily be adapted to suit the season. This is my food diary of sorts and I hope you enjoy cooking the recipes as much as I do.

Why eat with the seasons?

In days gone by, we ate only what was in season because nothing else was available to us. Before the invention of refrigerators, seasonal eating was a necessity; it was a time of limited storage and transport facilities, and seasonal labour forces. Nowadays we can buy whatever we want from the supermarket whenever we want to. Apples, asparagus and aubergines are on our shelves all year round and only one in ten people in the UK can identify when fruit and vegetables are in season. We're a bit out of touch with what we eat, it would seem.

But what exactly is seasonal eating? Put simply, it's eating fruit and vegetables harvested in the UK at certain times of the year. When you're in sync with the seasons, you'll know that you can buy Jerusalem artichokes in January and that apples are around in the autumn. You'll probably start to look forward to certain times of the year, say strawberry season, and decide that it's better to wait until the sweet and juicy ones appear instead of eating them all year round.

Maybe I'm living in a middle class bubble (I like to think not), but the appearance of new season broad beans or tomatoes at my local supermarket or greengrocer really does get me excited. But there are also some practical reasons for eating with the seasons.

In recent years, there has been a shift back to buying locally grown produce. Campaigners, food writers and chefs advocate seasonal eating because it can have a positive impact on the environment and local communities, and it tastes better.

At the time of writing, Britain is preparing to leave the European Union. When this happens, access to imported foods might become more difficult, and so seasonal eating will become more important than ever.

Our increasing demand for courgettes in February and radishes in December comes at a price. Here are just some of the reasons why it's better to eat seasonally.

- ### The environment

  Seasonal produce generally has a lower environmental impact because it requires lower levels of heating, lighting, pesticides and fertilisers than at other times of the year. Eating fruit and vegetables that have been grown in the UK reduces the energy needed to transport them from other countries – 26 per cent of all carbon emissions come from food production – so eating British asparagus in May uses less food mileage than buying what's flown in from South America. The same goes for products that we can never realistically grow in the UK: oranges shipped from Spain use far less energy than those from California.

- ### Cost

  Perhaps the biggest benefit of eating seasonally is that you'll save money on food. Because food in season is usually in abundance and has less distance to travel, it's cheaper. It costs less for farmers and distribution companies to harvest and get to the supermarket or greengrocer, which means that a British tomato bought in peak harvest season in August will cost less than one bought in January. And it's not only cheaper at the big supermarkets – if you can, shopping at your local greengrocer, farm shop or farmers' market can be just as cost effective. It's also better value for money because of the freshness, taste and quality of what you get.

- ### Nutrition and taste

  Because seasonal produce is fresher, it tends to be tastier and more nutritious. Eating seasonally means that you can enjoy fruit and vegetables that haven't had time to lose their taste or their health benefits by sitting in a shipping container – although fruit and vegetables produced locally, for example, bought from a farmers' market, are sometimes fresher than what you'll find at the supermarket. Eating with the seasons is also a good way to introduce some variety into your diet and helps you to get your five-a-day.

- ### Reconnect with nature – and your body

  Without wanting to sound too woo woo, eating seasonally allows us to reconnect with nature's cycles and the passing of time. Different food grows depending on how warm or cold it is and is in sync with what our bodies need at different times of year. That's why we want salads in the summer, then when it's cold we crave comforting stews and soups. Juicy summer fruits provide extra beta-carotenes and carotenoids to help protect against sun damage, while sprouts and kale are full of vitamin C for fighting winter's colds and flu.

- Local economy

  Eating with the seasons can support British producers and the local economy but in 2012, only 23% of the fruit and vegetables we bought were home grown. Unless you're after blood oranges or pineapples, by shopping seasonally you should usually be able to buy British. When you choose to buy locally grown food you support a diverse food economy; keeping more money in the local economy as well as supporting jobs in farming and food production. There is less time and distance between the grower and the buyer, often referred to as the field to fork journey. Whether you buy direct or at a local outlet, you're providing a market for local producers where they can get a fair price.

At the end of the day, let's not get too sniffy about seasonal eating, especially when millions of people in the UK, one of the richest countries in the world, are forced to use food banks. What farmers call the hungry gap, when in early spring, there is little fresh produce available, is a reality for many people here in Britain – and across the world – every month of the year. Malnutrition is as much if not more of a problem than obesity (and they often go hand in hand), and in 2018, studies showed that only 31 per cent of adults ate the recommended five portions of fruit and vegetables a day – with just 18 per cent of children doing the same. There are a multitude of reasons for this (food deserts for one), but it is possible to cook and eat fruit and vegetables in a way that's easy, inexpensive and tasty.

Eating seasonally is generally better, but we must be realistic. It's impossible for everything that you buy to come from the UK and there is an argument that it's better to import tomatoes grown in the heat of Spain rather than growing them in heated greenhouses in the UK. Unless climate change significantly changes the weather in the UK (this is a possibility and I shouldn't tempt fate), we will always buy imported bananas, citrus fruits and other exotic fruits, although better to buy them from Spain or Italy rather than those that have travelled much further from Africa, America or Australia. A lot has been said about the carbon footprint of avocados, so if you can, buy ones grown in Spain rather than those that hail from Chile or Mexico.

It's all about being more mindful about what you buy and put on your plate. I'm not an expert on growing or producing fruit and vegetables and this is a basic guide to eating with the seasons. It's not about being perfect, puritanical or

prescriptive about eating what's in season – and if you do buy seasonally, get it from wherever suits your budget and lifestyle. If you have to drive to your nearest farm but live within walking distance of a supermarket, put your trainers on! I hope this book will help you get a better understanding of the food seasons and what's in season and when.

A guide to eating seasonally

What's in season and when?

Seasons change and sometimes things will be available at slightly different times, but here's a rough guide to what's in season at different times of the year.

Some things, like carrots, onions and potatoes, are generally available all year round. Also available, and imported, are oranges, lemons, limes, grapefruit, bananas and avocado.

Spring	Summer	Autumn	Winter
Asparagus, broad beans, broccoli, carrots, cauliflower, chard, Jersey Royal potatoes, kale, leeks, lettuce, new potatoes, onions, parsnips, pumpkin, purple sprouting broccoli, radishes, rhubarb, rocket, spinach, spring greens, spring onions,	Artichokes, asparagus, aubergine, beetroot, blueberries, broad beans, broccoli, carrots, cherries, chillies, courgettes, cucumber, fennel, garlic, gooseberries, green beans, Jersey Royal potatoes, kohlrabi, lettuce, mangetout, new potatoes, onions,	Apples, artichokes, aubergine, beetroot, blackberries, broccoli, butternut squash, carrots, cauliflower, celeriac, celery, chard, chicory, courgettes, cucumber, damsons, elderberries, fennel, garlic, gooseberries, Jerusalem artichokes, kale,	Apples, beetroot, Brussels sprouts, blood oranges★, broccoli, carrots, cauliflower, celeriac, celery, chard, chestnuts, chicory, Jerusalem artichokes, kale, leeks, mushrooms, onions, parsnips, pears, pineapple★, pomegranate★, potatoes,

swede, turnips, samphire, sorrel, sugarsnap peas, watercress	peas, radishes, raspberries, rhubarb, rocket, runner beans, samphire, shallots, sorrel, spinach, strawberries, sugarsnap peas, sweetcorn, peppers, plums, tomatoes, turnips, watercress	kohlrabi, leeks, lettuce, marrow, mushrooms, new potatoes, onions, pak choi, parsnips, pears, plums, pumpkin, radishes, red cabbage, rocket, runner beans, salsify, samphire, shallots, sorrel, squash, swede, sweetcorn, sweet potatoes, sweetcorn, tomatoes, turnips, watercress	pumpkin, purple sprouting broccoli, radicchio, red cabbage, rhubarb, salsify, satsumas★, Savoy cabbage, shallots, squash, swede, turnips
Herbs: basil, chives, dill, sorrel basil, chives, coriander, dill, oregano, mint, nasturtium, parsley (curly), rosemary, sage, sorrel, tarragon	**Herbs:** basil, chives, coriander, dill, elderflowers, oregano, mint, nasturtium, parsley (curly), parsley (flat-leafed), rosemary, sage, sorrel, tarragon, thyme	**Herbs:** chives, coriander, oregano, mint, parsley (curly), parsley (flat-leafed), rosemary, sage, sorrel, thyme	

★ Imported

Getting the most out of your fruit and vegetables: a guide to nutrients

It's important to eat a varied diet when you decide to eat vegan, just as it is when you're a meat eater or vegetarian. I'm not going to tell you everything you need for a balanced diet, although you can find that in *The Occasional Vegan*, but I have put together a list of seasonal fruits and vegetables with the most health benefits.

The nutrients we need:

Vitamin A

Helps your immune system fight illness and infection, and keeps your eyes and skin healthy.

Vitamin B

There are many different types of vitamin B, which your body uses to release energy, maintain a healthy nervous system and keep your skin looking bright. It's possible to get all the different types from a vegan diet, although B12 can be tricky as it's only found naturally in foods from animal sources. Most dieticians recommend that vegans should take a vitamin B12 supplement.

Vitamin C

Helps to protect cells, maintains healthy skin, blood vessels, bones and cartilage and helps with wound healing.

Vitamin D

The body needs vitamin D to regulate the amount of calcium and phosphate in the body as these keep bones, teeth and muscles healthy. From April to the end of September, the majority of people in the UK should be able to get all the vitamin D they need from sunlight on their skin. The rest of the time it can be beneficial to take a supplement, but check the label as some forms of vitamin D contain lanolin which comes from sheep's wool.

Vitamin K

This is needed for blood clotting as it helps wounds heal properly and it also helps to keep bones healthy.

Calcium

We need this for strong and healthy bones and teeth, and contrary to popular belief, it's not only found in dairy.

Fibre

An important part of a healthy balanced diet as it can help prevent heart disease, diabetes, and some cancers, and can also improve digestive health.

Iron

Essential for the production of red blood cells.

Magnesium

Important for normal bone structure in the body and helps with muscle and nerve function, regulating blood pressure, and supporting the immune system.

Potassium

Helps to maintain a healthy blood pressure and is also important for the normal functioning of the nervous system.

Protein

We need protein so that the body can grow and repair itself.

Zinc

Needed for immune function, wound healing, growth and development.

The most nutritious fruits and vegetables

All fruits and vegetables are healthy, but some are especially good for you…

Apples – vitamins A and C, fibre, potassium (autumn, winter)
Asparagus – vitamins A, C and K, fibre, potassium, iron, calcium, protein and zinc (spring, summer)
Beetroot – vitamin C, fibre, iron, potassium (summer, autumn, winter)
Blackberries – vitamins A, C and K, fibre (autumn)
Blueberries – vitamin C, calcium, fibre, magnesium, zinc (summer)
Broccoli – iron, calcium, vitamins B, C and K, potassium, protein, fibre (spring, summer, autumn, winter)
Brussels sprouts – calcium, vitamin C, protein, fibre (winter)
Carrots – vitamin A, beta-carotene (spring, summer, autumn, winter)
Cauliflower – vitamins B6,C and K, fibre, magnesium, potassium and protein (spring, autumn, winter)
Kale – vitamins A, B6, C and K, calcium, iron, potassium, magnesium and zinc (spring, autumn, winter)

Mushrooms – vitamins B and D, fibre, protein, selenium and zinc (autumn, winter)

Onions – vitamins B6 and C, potassium (spring, summer, autumn, winter)

Peas – vitamins A, C and K, fibre, iron, protein and zinc (spring, summer)

Potatoes – vitamins B6 and C, fibre, magnesium and potassium (spring, summer, autumn, winter)

Pumpkin and squash – vitamins A, C and E, beta-carotene, calcium, fibre, magnesium and potassium (autumn, winter)

Raspberries – vitamins C and K, fibre, iron, magnesium and potassium (summer)

Rhubarb – vitamins C and K, calcium, fibre, potassium (spring, summer, winter)

Spinach – vitamins A, B6, C, E and K, calcium, folic acid, iron, magnesium, protein (summer)

Strawberries – vitamins C and E, iron, magnesium and potassium (summer)

Tomatoes – vitamins C and K, lycopene, potassium (summer, autumn)

Watercress – vitamins A, C and K, calcium, iron, magnesium, potassium and protein (spring, summer, autumn)

Where to buy

Buying in season gives you more taste and is better value for money. Organic fruit and vegetables are great but if you can't afford them, your local greengrocer or supermarket stock a range of cheap and plentiful produce. You can also visit farmers' markets or join a veg box scheme where you have fresh, locally grown produce delivered to your home every week.

A well-stocked kitchen

Once your kitchen is stocked, shopping shouldn't be expensive. Seasonal fruit and vegetables are cheap and plentiful, and beans, pulses, rice and other grains cost pennies. You can buy big bags of pulses for next to nothing in all supermarkets – or at your nearest Asian supermarket where they'll be even cheaper. Tins of chickpeas and other pulses are also inexpensive, whether from the supermarket or an international store. Visit your local pound or bargain shops where you can often find things like quinoa, nuts, seeds and dried fruit at a fraction of the price you'd pay at the supermarket.

Where to keep your fruit and vegetables

The cupboard

Root vegetables grow in dark places so it makes sense to keep potatoes, carrots, parsnips, beetroot and other roots in the cupboard.

The fruit bowl

It's not just for fruit. Keep some of your vegetables at room temperature for optimal flavour.

Things to put in the fruit bowl include apples, oranges, bananas, tomatoes, peppers, avocados, aubergines, chillies, garlic, lemons and limes, root ginger.

The fridge

Keep unwaxed lemons and limes (these go off more quickly if you leave them in the fruit bowl), cucumber, salad leaves, celery, carrots, mushrooms, broccoli and cauliflower in the fridge.

Fresh herbs like flat leaf parsley, rosemary, thyme, mint, basil, sage and coriander – or grow your own on the windowsill. You can keep herbs and greens for longer by rolling them up in damp paper towels and placing them in freezer bags with the seals left slightly open.

Tools and equipment

You'll need a few kitchen essentials for cooking simple – and more elaborate – meals. With all of these, buy the best you can afford.

Knives – you'll need a fairly large chef's knife (about 17.5-20cm/7-8 inches), a smaller knife (15cm/6 inches) and a bread knife. It's useful to have a knife sharpener, too.
Chopping boards
A box grater
Kitchen tongs
Saucepans – you'll need small, medium and large ones
Frying pans – buy non-stick
A casserole – buy a flame and heatproof one if you can so that it can go on the hob and in the oven
Roasting and baking trays
A sieve
A silicone whisk
A vegetable peeler
Mixing bowls
Pestle and mortar
Cake tins (buy non-stick if you can, so that you don't have to grease them)
Food processor – this isn't essential but it will save you time in the kitchen

Hand blender – if you can't afford a food processor or have little room in your kitchen, get one of these: they're inexpensive and are great for blending soups and sauces. Weighing scales – Again, these aren't essential if you're a fairly experienced cook as you can generally judge how much of the ingredients you need to use, but you will need them for baking as precision is key. I find that digital scales are always more accurate.

Oven temperatures and weights

All ovens are different so when following a recipe, you may find that you will need to adjust times and temperatures ever so slightly. I prefer to use an electric oven as the heat is distributed more evenly through the oven meaning that cooking is easier – and that's what I've used for all of the recipes in this book, so if you have a gas or electric fan oven, use this rough guide to oven temperatures when cooking.

Electricity °C	Electricity (fan) °C	Gas mark	Fahrenheit (F)
110	90	¼	225
120	100	¼	250
140	120	1	275
150	130	2	300
160	140	3	320
180	160	4	350
190	170	5	375
200	180	6	400
220	200	7	425
230	210	8	450
240	220	9	475

A guide to measurements

Conversion charts

Metric	Imperial
5g	¼ oz
8/10g	⅓ oz
15g	½ oz
20g	¾ oz
25g	1 oz
30/35g	1¼ oz
40g	1½ oz
50g	2 oz
60/70g	2½ oz
75/85/90g	3 oz
100g	3½ oz
110/120g	4 oz
125/130g	4½ oz
135/140/150g	5 oz
170/175g	6 oz
200g	7 oz
225g	8 oz
250g	9 oz
265g	9½ oz
275g	10 oz
300g	11 oz
325g	11½ oz
350g	12 oz
375g	13 oz

Dry weights

Metric	Imperial
400g	¼ oz
425g	⅓ oz
450g	½ oz
475g	¾ oz
500g	1 oz
550g	1¼ oz
600g	1½ oz
625g	2 oz
650g	2½ oz
675g	3 oz
700g	3½ oz
750g	4 oz
800g	4½ oz
850g	5 oz
900g	6 oz
950g	7 oz
1kg	8 oz
1.1kg	9 oz
1.25kg	9½ oz
1.3/1.4kg	10 oz
1.5kg	11 oz
1.75/1.8kg	11½ oz
2kg	12 oz

Liquids

Metric	Imperial	Cups
15ml	½fl oz	1 tbsp
20ml	¾fl oz	
30ml	1fl oz	⅛ cup
60ml	2fl oz	¼ cup
75ml	2½fl oz	
90ml	3fl oz	⅓ cup
100ml	3½fl oz	
120ml	4fl oz	½ cup
135ml	4½fl oz	
160ml	5fl oz	⅔ cup
180ml	6fl oz	¾ cup
210ml	7fl oz	
240ml	8fl oz	1 cup
265ml	9fl oz	
300ml	10fl oz	1¼ cups
350ml	12fl oz	1½ cups
415ml	14fl oz	
480ml	16fl oz / 1 pint	2 cups
530ml	18fl oz	2¼ cups
1 litre	32fl oz	4 cups

Meals for every season

These are the sorts of meals that follow the seasons – and the weather!

- A spring lunch: asparagus and pine nut puff pastry tart, spring potatoes with watercress pesto, stir-fried purple sprouting broccoli with satay sauce, rhubarb and polenta cake

- A summer barbeque: smashed cucumber and mint salad, tomato and corn salad, summer berry and coconut milk ice lollies, strawberry and basil sling

- A picnic in the park: asparagus salad with chickpeas, giant couscous and pistachios, pickled radishes, pea and samphire parcels with broad bean dip, lemon and thyme loaf

- Bonfire Night: creamy mushroom soup, jump for joy salad, beetroot ketchup, spiced parsnip cake with walnut frosting

- Christmas Day: parsnip, pecan and polenta loaf, roasted Jerusalem artichokes, jewelled red cabbage, sticky toffee apple pudding

- A chilly winter's day: French onion soup, spaghetti carbonara with creamy cauliflower sauce, root vegetable shepherd's pie, kohlrabi, celeriac and apple casserole

The recipes

Spring

I spend much of the winter months waiting for the spring. After day after day of cold and dark, I long for light and new beginnings. Springtime for me is lambs frolicking, fresh shoots and lighter evenings as the clocks go forward. It's still cold, but not as bitterly so as the winter months – although we sometimes see snow in March, or even in April.

It's the season for asparagus, purple sprouting broccoli, radiant radishes and rhubarb, watercress and, of course, spring greens.

In season now…

Asparagus, broad beans, broccoli, carrots, cauliflower, chard, Jersey Royal potatoes, kale, leeks, lettuce, new potatoes, onions, parsnips, pumpkin, purple sprouting broccoli, radishes, rhubarb, rocket, spinach, spring greens, spring onions, swede, turnips, samphire, sorrel, sugarsnap peas, watercress.

Welsh rarebit

Although it's still cold at this time of year, I have always been resolute in my belief that March marks the beginning of spring. It's David's Day, a day for daffodils and the patron saint of Wales. I write at a café, sipping oat milk flat whites and tapping away at my MacBook, a typical millennial, but only just — my mid-thirties are fast approaching. Walking home through Swansea city centre, I pass a crowd of girls dressed in traditional Welsh costumes dancing to a man bellowing out Elvis Presley hits. I'm bemused, but I later read that Elvis allegedly had Welsh roots. Who knew?

I make Welsh rarebit for dinner, so called because the English were mocking us. Rarebit is a corruption of the word rabbit, while "Welsh" was once used as an insult — for example, not having the money to eat rabbit. No bunnies are hurt in this recipe: I use cauliflower to make a creamy sauce and it works rather well.

Under 20 minutes | Serves 2

Ingredients

- 150g cauliflower, cut into florets
- 1 leek, trimmed and sliced
- 1 tbsp oil
- 150ml oat milk
- 1 tsp cornflour or plain flour
- 1 tsp wholegrain mustard
- 2–3 dashes of vegan Worcestershire sauce (try Biona)
- 2 tbsp nutritional yeast
- The juice of 1 lemon
- Salt and pepper
- 4 slices of wholegrain bread

Boil the cauliflower for 10–12 minutes, until tender, then drain and return to the pan. Meanwhile, fry the leeks in the oil for 6–7 minutes, until soft and translucent.

Mash the cauliflower using a potato masher or use a hand-held blender to blitz. Add the leeks (leave a few for the garnish) and all the other ingredients to the pan and stir over a low heat for a minute or two. Turn on the grill and toast the bread on one side. Turn over and divide the mixture between the four slices, making sure to spread evenly. Toast for 2–3 minutes, until bubbling, then garnish with the remaining slices of leeks and serve, perhaps with an extra dash of Worcestershire sauce.

Leek, kale and hazelnut pasta with pesto

I'm working in Cardiff today and although the sky is brilliantly blue, it's cold. By the time I leave the office it's dark, and back in Swansea, I walk home from the train station trussed up in my winter coat and scarf.

It's one of those evenings when I crave something warm and nourishing to eat even though I can't muster up much energy to cook. Luckily I've got everything I need to make a quick pasta dish with a silky sauce and crunchy hazelnuts. Ignoring Bobbie's cries for kale, I pour a glass of wine, curl up on the sofa with my dinner and zone out in front of the TV.

Under 20 minutes | Serves 2

Ingredients

— 150g wholewheat pasta
— 2 tbsp olive oil
— 1 large leek, ends removed and sliced
— 2 cloves garlic, peeled and crushed
— 2 large handfuls kale
— The juice of 1 lemon
— 50g hazelnuts
— Salt and pepper

Boil the pasta for 8-10 minutes. Meanwhile, fry the leeks and garlic in a little olive oil for 2-3 minutes, until soft. Add the kale and a little water and squeeze over the lemon juice and salt. Place the lid on the pan and cook for 2 minutes. Add the hazelnuts, cook for another 2 minutes and turn off the heat. Now blend the kale, hazelnuts, olive oil, salt and pepper and lemon juice. Add a little water. Drain the cooked pasta and add to the pan with the leeks and kale and stir through the pesto.

Pasta with wild garlic pesto

One Sunday afternoon, we drive to the Gower where the air is thick with the smell of wild garlic, and I get picking. Foraging is easy and it'll cost you nothing, although don't pick from private land without permission and only take as much as you intend to use. Make sure that you don't pick lily-of-the-valley, which looks similar but doesn't smell of garlic and is toxic.

At home, I make wild garlic pesto with mixed seeds for extra zinc, magnesium and omega oils – if you can't eat nuts, use more of the seeds. Wild garlic has a mellower flavour than garlic so I can afford to use a bit more of it, and because the flowers are edible, I add a few for decoration.

Under 15 minutes | Serves 2

Ingredients

- 200g spaghetti
- 5-6 leaves wild garlic
- 3 tbsp extra virgin olive oil
- 2 handfuls of pine nuts
- 1 handful seeds (optional)
- The juice of 1 lemon
- Salt and pepper
- Flowers to decorate

Boil a pan of salted water and cook the pasta for 8-10 minutes. Make the pesto by blending all of the ingredients, using a pestle and mortar or a stick blender. When the pasta is cooked, drain – but reserve a little water – and return to the pan. Add the water and the pesto and stir through, then divide between two bowls and serve.

Potato salad with watercress pesto

I t's one of those warm, early spring weekends, when one might be able to get away without wearing a coat. This morning, the sun streams through the blinds, whispering at me to get out of bed and make the most of the day.

I go for a walk with my friend Lindsey and invite her to stay for lunch. If we had a garden, today would be the day to eat al fresco, but instead, we open the French doors and let the sunshine stream in. I boil soft, velvety Jersey Royals and make a watercress pesto. I think of the late, great Nora Ephron, who said: "I have made a lot of mistakes falling in love, and regretted most of them, but never the potatoes that went with them."

Under 30 minutes | Makes one large bowl

Ingredients

- 700g–800g Jersey Royal potatoes, scrubbed and cut into half
- 50g hazelnuts
- A few leaves of fresh mint, stalks removed, plus extra for garnishing
- 3-4 tbsp extra virgin olive oil
- The juice of 2 lemons
- 1 clove garlic, peeled and crushed
- 3-4 large handfuls watercress
- A little oat milk
- Salt and pepper

Bring a large pan of water to the boil and cook the potatoes for 20-25 minutes, or until tender. Drain and return to the pan, then cover with cold water.

To make the pesto, put all the ingredients into a blender and pulse on a high setting for a minute or so. Add more oat milk or oil if you want a creamier consistency.

Drain the cooked potatoes and transfer to a large bowl, stir through the pesto and garnish with some extra mint leaves.

Super sunshine salad

As Mondays go, this one isn't too unpleasant, possibly because the sun is shining. I do some planning, a bit of work and manage to fit in a run. The state of the flat leaves a lot to be desired, however (who has time for housework?), so tonight, I want something easy for dinner, which will result in minimal washing up.

I make a bright and breezy salad in under ten minutes. It doesn't quite fill me with the joys of spring, but it's not far off, and it's fresh and vibrant in looks and personality. The dishes won't do themselves so I reluctantly pull on my rubber gloves and feel a lot calmer afterwards.

Under 10 minutes | Serves 2

Ingredients

- 1 head radicchio
- 1 bunch watercress
- 1 bunch spinach
- A handful of radishes, ends removed and sliced
- 1 x 400g can lentils, rinsed and drained
- 3 tbsp capers
- 1 pink grapefruit
- Sea salt
- 2 tbsp extra virgin olive oil
- Fresh dill, chopped
- Salt and pepper

Cut the pink grapefruit in half. Roughly chop the radicchio, watercress and spinach, put in a large bowl and squeeze over the juice from the half grapefruit. Add a little salt and the olive oil and massage the leaves. Add the lentils and radishes and the capers. Cut the remainder of the grapefruit into segments and add to the salad. Mix everything together and top with the chopped dill. Season with salt and pepper and serve.

Roasted leeks with swede and walnut dip

I like the bright, still mornings of early spring. The clocks have gone forward and it gets light before seven. On the days that I travel for work, I'm always surprised by how many people I see, in awe that they do this every day, when sometimes I'm still in pyjamas at ten.

I trudge to the train station past grey streets that have seen better days, clutching a still hot thermos of coffee. As I board the 7.59, I find a table seat and get out my laptop. As the train trundles towards Cardiff, I write or daydream or reply to texts. I usually think about dinner. It's Wednesday, and to mark the middle of the week, I'm going to make some Catalan-style roasted leeks with a creamy swede dip.

Under 1 hour | Serves 4

Ingredients

For the dip
- 1 large swede (or 400g), peeled and diced
- 3 tbsp olive oil
- Salt and pepper
- 150g walnuts
- 1 tsp spiced paprika
- 2 tsp smoked paprika
- The juice of 1 lemon
- A pinch of chilli flakes
- 100ml water

For the leeks
- 4 leeks, whole, ends removed
- 3 tbsp olive oil
- 2 tsp fennel seeds
- Salt and pepper

Preheat the oven to 200C. Put the chopped swede into a large ovenproof dish, drizzle over the olive oil and season. Place on the top shelf of the oven and roast for 30 minutes. Remove from the oven, add the walnuts and roast for a further 15–20 minutes, until the swede is tender and the walnuts are a dark brown colour.

While the swede is cooking, place the leeks on a large sheet of foil and drizzle over the olive oil, then add the fennel seeds and some salt and pepper. Wrap the foil around the leeks and put in the oven to roast for 30 minutes.

When the swede and walnuts are ready, remove from the oven and leave to cool slightly. Tip into a food processor, add the other ingredients and blitz. Remove the leeks from the oven, and carefully open the foil. Cut the leek in half, lengthways and divide onto four plates. Serve with the dip.

Rhubarb and polenta cake

Cardiff is covered in a carpet of pink blossom this morning, a very pretty distraction from intermittent rain showers and a bad night's sleep. There are too many thoughts in my head at the moment and they're keeping me awake at night. I've always been sensitive to the changing seasons, although I feel much freer when darkness doesn't set in at 4pm on the dot.

Thinking of pink, I drink my mid-morning coffee with a slice of cake made with new-season rhubarb. Despite their bright colour, these bittersweet stalks are just sharp enough to rouse your taste buds from their winter hibernation. It's completely gluten free if you use coconut flour, and the polenta provides a light and fluffy texture.

Under 50 minutes | Makes 1 medium cake

Ingredients

– ½ tsp apple cider vinegar
– 140ml plant milk
– 1 tbsp milled flax seeds
– The juice of 1 orange
– 400g rhubarb
– 100g plain or coconut flour
– 100g quick-cook polenta
– 100g caster sugar
– 1 tsp baking powder
– ½ tsp bicarbonate of soda
– 2 tbsp agave
– 1 tsp cinnamon
– ½ tsp vanilla extract
– 1 pinch salt
– 50ml rapeseed oil

Heat the oven to 180C. Grease a 9-inch springform cake tin. Place the chopped rhubarb in a saucepan with the orange juice, cinnamon and vanilla extract and stew over a medium heat for five minutes or until soft. Set aside to cool.

In a bowl, combine the flour, polenta, caster sugar, the baking powder, bicarb and salt and milk, and whisk. Add the rapeseed oil and mix again, then add the flax seeds and agave and whisk to combine.

Add the stewed rhubarb and combine with the mixture. Pour into the greased cake tin and bake for 25-30 minutes, or until a skewer comes out clean.

Garlicky rainbow chard with tahini

I t's been a busy few weeks and I'm looking forward to the four-day weekend that's coming up. I get home from Cardiff late, fully aware that last night's washing up is still sitting by the sink. I don't want to add to that pile, so a simple supper is needed.

I'm a sucker for a stir-fry and it's often my go-to when I'm tired, busy or feeling lazy. There's some rainbow chard in the fridge so I turn these lively leaves into a zippy and zesty dish. This most vibrant of vegetables is a good source of fibre, iron, calcium and vitamins A, C, and K – just the reviver I need after a long day.

Under 10 minutes | Serves 2

Ingredients

– 400g rainbow chard, tough ends removed and roughly chopped
– 2 tbsp sesame oil
– 2 cloves garlic, peeled and grated
– 1 tbsp soy sauce
– 1 inch ginger, peeled and grated
– The juice of 1 lime
– 3-4 tbsp tahini
– 1 tsp sesame seeds
– 1 tsp nigella seeds

Place a large frying pan or wok over a medium temperature and heat the sesame oil. Throw in the chopped chard, then add the garlic, soy sauce, ginger and lime juice and fry for about five minutes, until the leaves are wilted. Divide onto two plates and drizzle over the tahini then scatter over the sesame and nigella seeds.

Rhubarb and buckwheat with smoked tofu

Easter is late this year, and for me, the break is much needed. It's one of the hottest weekends of the year so far and we have a lovely day with chocolate for breakfast, a walk in the woods, a trip to Three Cliffs Bay, bluebells, and plenty of wild garlic to take home.

We get home in the early evening and it's still light. I think about what to eat and the bunch of rhubarb languishing in the salad drawer. I've recently learned that rhubarb and buckwheat belong to the same family so I decide to experiment – and dinner ends up being rather special. This, I suppose, is my version of fine dining.

Under 50 minutes | Serves 4

Ingredients

- 1 x 400g block firm tofu
- 4 stalks rhubarb, ends removed and sliced into 4-inch pieces
- 2 tsp coconut oil
- A whole bag of spinach
- 200g buckwheat
- 1 lime (juice)
- Half a jar of capers

For the marinade
- 3 tbsp soy sauce
- 1 tsp sea salt
- 2 tbsp maple syrup
- 2 tbsp sesame oil
- 1 tsp smoked paprika
- ½ tsp cinnamon

For the dressing
- 1 of the cooked stalks of rhubarb, chopped
- 3 tbsp tahini
- 2 handfuls spinach
- A handful of parsley
- 1 tbsp olive oil
- A pinch of sea salt

In a large dish, combine the marinade ingredients. Slice the tofu into four chunks and place in the dish, turning over so that each side is coated in the mixture. Leave for 10-15 minutes – or longer if possible.

Preheat the oven to 200C. In a large pan, heat the coconut oil over a high temperature. Place the tofu strips in the pan with a little of the marinade (keep the rest for later), add three of the rhubarb stalks, cut into pieces, and fry for about 5 minutes, turning occasionally. Transfer the tofu and the rhubarb to an ovenproof dish and pour over the rest of the marinade. Place on the top shelf of the oven and bake for 10–15 minutes.

Meanwhile, rinse and drain the buckwheat. Using the same pan, on a low, temperature toast the buckwheat for around 10 minutes or until slightly brown. Pour over the lime juice and salt and stir occasionally. In the same pan, cook the spinach until wilted. Add a little oil if necessary.

Quickly make the dressing by blending all the ingredients in a food processor or by using a hand-held blender.

Remove the tofu and rhubarb from the oven and divide onto four plates. Serve with the buckwheat and spinach, add a few capers to each plate, and drizzle over the dressing.

Stir-fried purple sprouting broccoli with satay sauce

Described by T.S. Eliot as the cruellest month, April's a big tease, coaxing us out of our coats with warm spring days and then quite literally putting a dampener on things with a sudden downpour. At the start of the month, I begin a new freelance project in Cardiff. The office is a stone's throw from the civic centre, which is awash with red tulips. The sky is brilliantly blue and I think back to childhood and long Saturday afternoons spent at the museum and its gardens.

As I walk along city streets, I think ahead to the summer months, dreaming of sun on bare skin. Pretty purple sprouting broccoli is already in season so I turn it into a simple side dish to eat as a snack before dinner. Frying the broccoli retains its crunch and a smooth satay sauce makes a great sidekick.

Under 15 minutes | Serves 2

Ingredients

– Half a packet of purple sprouting broccoli (or 8-10 florets)
– 1 tbsp sesame oil
– A splash of soy sauce
– The juice of half a lime

For the satay sauce
– 1 tbsp smooth peanut butter
– 1 tbsp sesame oil
– 1 tbsp soy sauce
– The juice of half a lime
– A pinch of chilli flakes

Heat the oil in a large frying pan or wok over a medium-high temperature. Add the broccoli, followed by the soy sauce and lime juice and stir-fry for 7-8 minutes until slightly tender.

Meanwhile, mix together the ingredients for the satay sauce, using a spoon. Serve with the broccoli.

Pickled radishes

It's very nearly the end of April, and as it's the school holidays, we go to Cardiff to see the Leonardo Da Vinci exhibition at the National Museum. It's a quick visit — eleven-year-olds get bored easily — but I'm impressed, although in all honesty, I'm more enamoured by an oil painting of Tom Jones.

Before we head home (and onwards to Ikea), I pop into Cardiff Market where part of my haul includes several bunches of radishes, reduced at the end of the day. As we drive back, the sky is awash with the prettiest pink sunset I've seen in a while and it seems fitting to make something with the brightly hued radishes in my bag.

Under 30 minutes | Makes 1 jar

Ingredients

- 150g radishes
- 150ml rice vinegar
- 1 tbsp sesame oil
- ½ tsp mustard seeds
- ½ tsp coriander seeds
- ½ tsp black onion seeds (optional)
- A generous pinch of salt

Trim and finely slice the radishes. In a large bowl, mix the vinegar, oil and spices. Add the radishes and toss together, then leave to marinade for 10-15 minutes. Add to a jar, cover with a lid, and give it a good shake before serving. This will keep in the fridge for a few days. If you'd like it to last longer, you'll need to sterilise the jar.

Asparagus salad with chickpeas, giant couscous and pistachios

We've reached the end of what farmers call the hungry gap, when, in early spring, there is little fresh produce available. That period is well and truly over, with greens lining up on the shelves of our greengrocers: watercress, cucumber, leeks, spring greens, and my favourite, asparagus.

British asparagus season is short but sweet, but these stubborn little spears are a hardy lot and will generally stick around in the salad drawer for a good week or so.

The sun's out and I make a quick and easy salad with asparagus as the star of the show and zesty lemon and salty pistachios as its backing singers. It takes under ten minutes from pan to plate, which is handy as I'm heading out to meet friends later this evening.

Under 10 minutes | Serves 2-3

Ingredients

– 100g giant couscous
– 1 can (400g) chickpeas, rinsed and drained
– 1 packet of asparagus (or 7–8 spears)
– Half a bag of spinach
– 2–3 handfuls pistachios, shelled
– The juice of 1 lemon
– 2–3 tbsp extra virgin olive oil
– Salt and pepper to season

Using a sieve, rinse and drain the couscous then add to a pan of salted boiling water and cook for 5–6 minutes. At the same time, in a separate pan, boil or steam the asparagus for 5–6 minutes.

In a large bowl, mix the chickpeas and spinach and massage with 2 tablespoons of olive oil and half the lemon juice. Season with salt and pepper. Drain the couscous and add to the bowl (its warmth will gently wilt the spinach leaves) and do the same with the asparagus. Top with the pistachios and dress with the remainder of the lemon juice and olive oil. Season with salt and pepper and serve.

Asparagus and pine nut puff pastry tart

I t's not often that sunny weather and a quieter spell of work happen at the same time, but this week, time is on my side. Swansea comes into its own in the sun. I wish it was always like this.

I spend most of the week walking along the beach, reading in the park and sitting in coffee shops, replying to the odd email. By Friday, I'm a bit bored so I decide to make myself busy in the kitchen. As is often the case in May, I have a bunch of asparagus in the fridge, plus a roll of puff pastry so I make a simple spring tart for dinner, which we enjoy with boiled Jersey Royals and a chilled bottle of Sauvignon Blanc.

Under 1 hour | Serves 4

Ingredients

– 8-10 asparagus spears, depending on the size of your pie dish
– 1 puff pastry sheet
– 1 x 400g can cannellini beans, drained
– The juice of 1 lemon
– 2 tsp Dijon mustard
– 2-3 tsp fresh dill
– 2 tsp salt
– A grinding of black pepper
– 4 tbsp olive oil
– 2 tsp capers
– 2-3 tbsp pine nuts

Take the puff pastry sheet out of the fridge. Preheat the oven to 180C. Fry or sauté the asparagus spears in a little oil for 5 minutes.

Using a stick blender, blend the cannellini beans, lemon juice, mustard, salt and pepper, dill, olive oil and capers.

Grease a rectangular pie dish (I use a 10 x 8 inch dish) with a little oil – or use a sheet of greaseproof paper – and then place the sheet of puff pastry across the base. Spoon over the bean mixture and layer the asparagus spears on top. Bake for 20 minutes, then remove from the oven, scatter over the pine nuts and bake for another 20-25 minutes, until the pastry is golden.

Smoked carrot and cashew cheese toasts

It's the first bank holiday in May – we get two this month – and I spend a lazy weekend catching up on sleep, reading and drinking coffee. There's a walk, of course, and we go to Clyne Gardens, which at this time of year is a flush of colour, and I go in search of bluebells but can't find any; it must be too early.

When we get home, I potter in the kitchen making smoked carrots and a cashew spread. Carrots are in season all year round, but there's something light and spring-like about these moreish morsels. We eat it on toast but these are also good as canapés with drinks or spread thickly on a bagel, New York style.

Under 45 minutes | Makes enough for about 24 toasts

Ingredients

For the smoked carrot
– 2 large carrots, peeled
– 500ml water
– 2 tsp sea salt
– 3 Lapsang Souchong teabags
– 1 tbsp soy sauce
– 1 tbsp sesame oil

For the cashew 'cheese'
– 200g cashews
– 300ml water
– The juice of 1 lemon
– 2 tbsp yeast flakes
– 50ml oat milk
– A generous pinch of salt
– Freshly ground pepper
– Good white bread

Cut the carrots into ribbons with a vegetable peeler and set aside. Pour 500ml water into a large saucepan with the salt and bring to the boil. Add the carrot ribbons and teabags and remove from the heat. Leave to steep for at least 20 mins until the mixture is cold and the ribbons have softened. Pour into a smaller container or jar, add the soy sauce and sesame oil, then chill until needed.

To make the cream cheese, put the cashews in a bowl and pour over the water. Leave to soak for 30 minutes. Drain the cashew nuts, then tip into a food processor and add the lemon juice, oat milk, salt and pepper and yeast flakes. Blitz then taste – add more salt or oat milk if needed.

Drain the carrot ribbons, discard the brine and the tea bags and pat dry with kitchen paper or a clean tea towel.

Toast the bread and cut into slices. Spread with the cashew nut cheese and top with the carrots. Serve with a little ground black pepper and a squeeze of lemon juice.

Spaghetti with spring greens, spinach, lemon, walnuts and breadcrumbs

D oes spring fever really exist? I feel a bit all over the place at the moment as I scribble in notebooks and try to structure my scattered thoughts. I want to do too much, perhaps, but that often means that I don't start anything. Today wasn't as productive as I'd have liked, and for some reason, it's really bothering me.

Life sometimes feels like one long to-do list, but I'm a firm believer that carbs will fix almost anything, so tonight I soothe myself with comfort food, wine and a double bill of Big Little Lies. I make spaghetti with spring greens, lemon zest, walnuts, breadcrumbs and lots of garlic – and I feel better. Tomorrow's a new day, after all.

Under 20 minutes | Serves 2

Ingredients

– 2 tbsp olive or rapeseed oil
– 200g wholewheat spaghetti
– 2 cloves garlic, peeled and crushed
– 2 slices of stale white or brown bread, roughly grated
      so that it resembles breadcrumbs
– One head of spring greens or cabbage, finely sliced or shredded
– The juice of 1 unwaxed lemon, plus zest
– Half a bag of spinach
– 50ml oat milk
– 50g walnuts, halved
– Salt and pepper

Bring a pan of salted water to the boil and cook the spaghetti for 8-10 minutes. In a large frying pan, heat the oil over a medium temperature and fry half the garlic and breadcrumbs, then remove from the pan and set aside. Add the spring greens or cabbage to the pan with the rest of the garlic and breadcrumbs, plus the lemon juice and zest, then add the spinach, oat milk and walnuts. Cook for 2-3 minutes, then drain the spaghetti and add, with a little of the water, to the pan. Stir and warm through for a minute, adding a little more milk if needed. Divide between two dishes and top with the fried garlic and breadcrumbs and a little extra lemon zest.

Carrot and coriander stew

We spend a sunny May bank holiday weekend in Winchester. It's good to get away, see friends and explore a chocolate-box-pretty city, but we arrive home tired and hungry. It's late and the fridge is almost empty except for a few carrots lurking at the bottom of the salad drawer.

I make a simple carrot and coriander stew with red lentils and a squeeze of lime. I'm not a huge fan of fresh coriander, which reminds me a bit of soap, so I grind some coriander seeds for a still fragrant but subtler taste. By now, it's raining, typical for a British bank holiday, and the stew is warming and comforting. We watch television, thankful that tomorrow is another day off work.

Under 40 minutes | Serves 2-3

Ingredients

– 2 tsp coconut oil
– 2 tsp coriander seeds, crushed
– 1 tsp mustard seeds, crushed
– 1 leek, ends removed and diced
– 5-6 carrots (around 400g), diced
– 1 inch ginger, peeled and grated
– 2 cloves garlic, peeled and crushed
– 1 small red chilli, finely chopped
– 150g red lentils, rinsed and drained
– 400ml hot vegetable stock
– 150ml coconut milk (from a carton)
– 3 tbsp tomato purée
– The juice of 1 lime
– Fresh coriander (optional)

In a large pan, melt the oil over a medium temperature then add the coriander and mustard seeds and fry for 2 minutes. Add the chopped leek and carrots and fry for 5-6 minutes, then add the ginger, garlic and chilli and fry for a further 3 minutes. Now add the lentils and the stock and stir through the tomato purée, then clamp on a lid and simmer for 20 minutes, stirring occasionally. Add the milk and cook for another 5 minutes. When cooked, stir through the lime juice and serve with rice plus some chopped coriander, if using.

Spring vegetable frittata with zhoug

I t's the last day of May and grey clouds slowly spread across the sky in Swansea, threatening rain. Work is back up to speed and it's been a busy week at work, so today I sleep in, make a smoothie and set about catching up on all the things that I've let slide.

The clouds still haven't broken, but it's humid. By mid-afternoon, I'm starving so I take some sad-looking vegetables from the fridge and make a tasty spring vegetable frittata with chickpea flour. I whizz up some zhoug, a sweet and spicy Yemeni sauce, to have with it. It hits the spot and fuels me just enough to carry on working for another few hours.

Under 25 minutes | Serves 1

Ingredients

For the frittata
- 3 tbsp rapeseed or coconut oil
- 3-4 spears asparagus, ends removed and sliced
- 4-5 radishes, ends removed and sliced
- 2-3 handfuls spinach
- 120g chickpea/gram flour
- ½ tsp dried mint
- 1 tsp sumac
- ½ tsp dried thyme
- 2 tbsp nutritional yeast
- The juice of half a lemon
- Salt and pepper
- 250ml water

For the zhoug
- 2 handfuls watercress
- 50g coriander, leaves and stalks, chopped
- 25g flat leaf parsley, chopped
- 1 clove garlic, peeled
- 1 green chilli, deseeded and roughly chopped
- ½ tsp brown sugar
- 1 tsp ground cumin
- The juice of half a lemon
- 2-3 tbsp olive oil

Heat 1 tbsp oil over a medium heat in a non-stick, heatproof frying pan and fry the vegetables for 5 minutes. Transfer to a plate and set aside for later. In a large bowl, mix together the flour, salt and pepper, herbs and spices, and the nutritional yeast and combine. Add the lemon juice and gradually add the water, whisking constantly.

Preheat the grill to a medium temperature. Heat the rest of the oil in the pan over a medium pan. Pour in the batter, making sure that it reaches all sides of the pan, and quickly spread over the cooked vegetables. Fry for 2-3 minutes then place on the top shelf of the grill and cook for another 2-3 minutes, until golden.

Meanwhile, quickly make the zhoug. Blitz all the ingredients using a hand-held blender or in a food processor. Serve drizzled over the frittata.

Summer

As I get older, I'm starting to realise that, really, summer is my season. It gives me the footloose freedom I'd like to have all year round. Summer means bare legs, balmy evenings and barbeques on the beach. Coats and even cardigans are a distant memory and the air is warm when I step outside at night to put the rubbish out or call in the cat.

It's the season for broad beans, peas, tomatoes and summer's finest: sweet strawberries, cherries and raspberries.

In season now…

Artichokes, asparagus, aubergine, beetroot, blueberries, broad beans, beetroot, broccoli, carrots, cherries, chillies, courgettes, cucumber, fennel, garlic, gooseberries, green beans, jersey royal new potatoes, kohlrabi, lettuce, mangetout, onions, new potatoes, peas, radishes, raspberries, rhubarb, rocket, runner beans, samphire, shallots, sorrel, spinach, strawberries, sugarsnap peas, sweetcorn, peppers, plums, tomatoes, turnips, watercress.

Pancakes with blueberry compote and coconut cream

It's June, a month of weddings, gin and tonics enjoyed in the garden and slow summer days and evenings. It's a sunny Saturday, and the three of us are heading to the Hay Festival. I make pancakes for breakfast and a compote with early summer blueberries. I'm a nervous flipper but manage not to make too much of a hash of this and I enjoy it with a mug of coffee before we scramble to get ready to leave the house – time-keeping is not our strong point.

The festival, mecca for the middle classes, is very hot, especially under the marquee, and I soon have a headache. We have tickets to see Jaqueline Wilson, whose books I enjoyed as a child and which Seren now reads, and the audience of children and adults quietly fizzes with excitement. Perhaps they too will write children's books one day. There's no time to explore the town's many bookshops and I hope we'll return soon.

Under 20 minutes | Makes 2 large pancakes

Ingredients

- 160g chickpea/gram flour
- 1 ½ tsp baking powder
- 2 tbsp maple syrup
- 1 tsp cinnamon
- 200ml plant milk or water
- 2-3 tbsp oil

For the compote
- 200g fresh or frozen blueberries
- 45ml water
- 50g granulated sugar
- The juice of half a lemon
- 1 tsp vanilla extract

- Half a tin or packet of coconut cream

Mix the dry ingredients together and gradually add the water or milk and the maple syrup and stir until it has a thick, but pourable, consistency. Heat the oil in a non-stick pan over a medium heat (test if it's hot enough by dropping in a tiny bit of batter – it should sizzle) then pour in half the batter and cook, flipping over occasionally, for 3-4 minutes. Repeat with the rest of the batter.

To make the compote, combine the blueberries, water, sugar, vanilla extract and lemon juice in a small saucepan. Cook over a medium heat for about 10-15 mins. Serve warm or cold.

Serve with the compote and coconut cream.

Summer vegetable lasagne

I'm not in a rush to do anything at the moment. It's hot, work is winding down (a little bit, anyway) for the summer and I have a holiday on the horizon. I'm making the most of the long and light evenings and taking the time to cook at a leisurely pace.

It's a humid evening and I make a light and bright lasagne with a pea, courgette and mint base and a creamy cauliflower sauce. While it's cooking in the oven, I pour a glass of white wine and settle down with a book. When I hear screeching and growling, I rush to the window and see that Bobbie in a stand-off with the local bully, a large ginger tom cat. I shoo him away and peace is restored – and Bobbie is soon distracted by her own dinnertime.

1 hour 10 minutes | Serves 4-6 people

Ingredients

For the base
- 1 tbsp olive oil
- 1 large onion, peeled and diced
- 2 cloves garlic, peeled and crushed
- 500g peas, podded
- 2-3 small courgettes, diced
- 2 handfuls fresh mint
- The juice of 1 lemon
- 300-350ml vegetable stock
- Half a bag of spinach
- Salt and pepper

For the creamy sauce
- 1 large cauliflower (about 600g), broken into florets
- 400ml oat milk
- The juice of 1 lemon
- 2 tsp white miso paste
- 2 garlic cloves, peeled and crushed
- 4 tsp yeast flakes
- 1 tbsp cornflour or plain flour
- A grating of nutmeg (or ½ tsp ground)

- 1 pack of lasagne sheets

Bring a pan of salted water to the boil and boil the cauliflower florets for 12-14 minutes, or until tender. Drain, return to the pan and set aside.

In a large pan, fry the onions and garlic in the oil for 2 minutes, then add the courgettes and half the stock. Fry over a low heat for 5 minutes, then add the peas, the mint and the rest of the stock. Cook for 5-6 minutes, then add the spinach and cook for a further 2-3 minutes then turn off the heat.

Preheat the oven to 200C. To the pan with the cauliflower, add the rest of the ingredients and bring to the boil, stirring constantly. Mash the cauliflower or use a hand-held blender to blitz into a sauce.

In a 10 x 8 inch dish, pour over half the pea and courgette base and spread evenly. Pour over half the cauliflower sauce and spread evenly then layer over some lasagne sheets, making sure to cover all of the sauce. Add another layer of the base followed by a layer of the sauce.

Place on the top shelf of the oven and bake for 40-45 minutes, until the top is golden and crispy.

Lemon and thyme drizzle loaf

Today is overcast and muggy, a sunless Sunday, and this morning's attempt at running wasn't easy. I feel a bit defeated by exercise at the moment; for me, it's a question of mind over matter, but I can't seem to get my head to make my legs keep going.

To cheer myself up, I turn to baking. I make a lemon loaf with a twist – thyme. This is a cake for grown-ups, and as I predict, my fussy monkeys enjoy this until they discover the 'green bits'. If you too are not a fan of putting herbs in sweet things, you can leave out the thyme and make a lovely lemony cake all the same.

Under 1 hour | Makes 1 loaf

Ingredients

- 275g self-raising flour
- 1 tsp baking powder
- 200g caster sugar
- The juice of 2 large lemons
- 4–5 sprigs (or 2 tsp) of thyme, leaves only
- 50ml olive, rapeseed or vegetable oil, plus extra for greasing the tin
- 100ml plant milk
- 150ml cold water

Heat the oven to 200C. Sieve the flour and baking powder into a mixing bowl and then mix together with the sugar, lemon juice and thyme. Add the oil, milk and cold water, then mix until smooth.

Grease a 9×5-inch loaf tin and line with greaseproof paper, then pour the mixture into the tin. Bake for 35-40 minutes or until a skewer comes out clean. Cool in the tin for 10 minutes, then remove the cake and transfer it to a wire rack to cool. This will keep in an airtight container for a couple of days.

Risotto with broad beans

Freelancing, I've found, is forever a case of feast or famine. I've been worrying about how I'll pay my tax bill come January, but then, out of the blue, I get an email offering me some work and I'm invited to interview for a part-time job. I feel almost instant relief, my load lightened somewhat.

For tonight's dinner, I make a fresh and zesty risotto with broad beans – these pale green sleeves are abundant at this time of year – and I double pod the beans, which is always worth doing, despite the time it takes. It's easy to make but risotto requires a fair bit of stirring which, I discover, is rather soothing – meditative, almost.

Under 50 minutes | Serves 4

Ingredients

– 300g risotto rice
– 250g broad beans, double podded
– 1 leek, diced
– 2 cloves garlic, finely chopped
– 1 litre of vegetable stock
– 1 tbsp olive oil
– The juice of 1 lemon
– Fresh dill, finely chopped (optional)
– Freshly ground pepper

Heat the oil in a large pan, then add the leek and sauté for 3 minutes. Add the garlic and cook for a further 2 minutes. Using a sieve, rinse and drain the rice, then add to the pan. Mix well, coating each grain in oil – add a little extra if necessary. Add a ladleful of the hot stock to the rice and stir well. Bring to a simmer as the liquid is absorbed by the rice. Continue adding more stock, a ladleful at a time, letting the rice absorb it gradually; do this for about 15-20 minutes, until the rice is soft. Add the broad beans, lemon juice and black pepper and stir through. Cook for another 5 minutes, adding extra liquid if necessary.

Turn off the heat and stir through the chopped dill (if using) and serve with steamed asparagus, green vegetables or on its own.

Tomato and radish salad with freekeh, mint and coriander

I've been struggling to sleep and feel tired and grouchy as a result. I've always been a light sleeper and the slightest sound or movement can jerk me awake. I'm sleepless in Swansea and only coffee can cure me.

It's been a slow morning so far, and hoping that I'll have more get-up-and go after lunch, I make something simple but sustaining to eat. I use up some wares from a shopping trip in Cardiff earlier in the week (juicy tomatoes from Laura's and freekeh from Beanfreaks) in a sustaining salad. The fresh flavours temporarily lift me from my grey brain fog and I manage a couple of hours of writing before I admit defeat and curl up on the sofa for the rest of the afternoon.

Under 30 minutes | Serves 2

Ingredients

For the salad
– 100g freekeh
– Pinch of sea salt
– 1 tbsp olive oil
– Half a punnet of cherry tomatoes, halved
– Half a punnet of plum tomatoes, halved
– 8 radishes, sliced
– 3-4 handfuls spinach leaves
– Fresh mint
– Fresh coriander

For the dressing
– The juice of 1 and ½ lemons
– 1 tbsp extra virgin olive oil
– 1 tsp dried mint (or oregano)
– ½ tsp chilli flakes
– ½ tsp sea salt

Place the freekeh and 500ml of water in a saucepan, add the oil and salt, if using, and bring to the boil. Cook for 15-20 minutes until tender and drain and return to the pan. Add the spinach leaves so that they wilt, pour over the dressing and stir. Transfer to a bowl and add the tomatoes, radishes and mint and coriander. Serve.

Strawberry, avocado and mint salad

I
t looks as though summer's arrived and I've got the sunburn to prove it. Last week, we holidayed in Tavira, town of turmeric coloured tiles and violently pink salt flats. I've realised that all holidays follow a pattern: the stress as you scramble to get everything done before you jet off, the moment you settle in and switch off, and the sadness when you leave.

Back in Wales, it's still sunny and all I want to eat is salad. Tonight's supper is light but luscious and takes five minutes to put together. I can't cut into an avocado without Bobbie crying for a morsel; she loves the stuff and I always give in to her, especially as I feel bad about leaving her at the cattery while we were away.

Under 15 minutes | Serves 2

Ingredients

— Half a punnet of strawberries, hulled and sliced in half
— 2-3 big handfuls of spinach leaves
— 2 tbsp extra virgin olive oil
— 2 tbsp balsamic vinegar
— 1 large avocado, sliced
— 1 can (400g) chickpeas, rinsed and drained
— Half a head of broccoli, broken into florets
— A handful of flaked almonds (optional)
— A few fresh mint leaves, roughly chopped
— 2 tablespoons balsamic vinegar
— 1 tablespoon olive oil
— 1 tablespoon pomegranate molasses (optional)

Steam the broccoli for 4-5 minutes and allow to cool. Meanwhile, place the spinach leaves in a large bowl and massage with the olive oil and half the balsamic vinegar. Stir in the chickpeas and add the avocado and broccoli. Place the strawberries in a separate bowl and coat with the rest of the balsamic vinegar, then add to the salad. Sprinkle over the flaked almonds and the mint, then drizzle over the pomegranate molasses

Pea and samphire parcels with broad bean and mint dip

I rather like July, even if it does mean pink skin, insect bites and, as anyone working in a marketing or communications role in Wales knows – and dreads – the Royal Welsh Show. It's Monday and I take the afternoon off to see my sister. It's a beautifully warm day and we sit outside at an Italian café. As we catch up over coffee I get a phone call and am offered the part-time job that I interviewed for last month. I head home with a spring in my step. It looks like it will be a good month.

I celebrate with a gin and tonic and make some salty and lightly spiced pastries with samphire, which is always a treat. I stocked up on it when I saw it at the supermarket yesterday so I have plenty left over. The parcels are easy to make, as is the minty broad bean dip, and delicious, and I eat rather a lot of them.

Under 40 minutes | Makes about 18 parcels

Ingredients

For the samosas
– 1 x 270g pack ready-made
    filo pastry sheets
– 1 onion, peeled and finely diced
– 2 cloves garlic, peeled and minced
– 2 x 90g packs samphire
– 400g fresh peas, podded
– The juice of 1 lemon
– 2 tsp sumac
– ½ tsp cumin
– 1 tsp dried mint
– 1 tsp rapeseed or vegetable oil,
    plus extra for brushing

For the broad bean dip
– 300g broad beans, double podded
– 3-4 tbsp extra virgin olive oil
– A handful of fresh mint
– 2 tsp dried mint
– The juice of 1 lemon
– 1 tsp sea salt

Preheat the oven to 200C and line two baking trays with baking paper. Remove the pastry from the fridge.

Warm the oil in a medium-sized frying pan and add the garlic and onions. Fry for 1-2 minutes or until softened, then stir in the sumac, cumin and mint. Add the peas and samphire and fry for about 5 minutes.

Unroll the filo pastry so that all the sheets are directly on top of each other in a block. Slice the pastry lengthways into three rectangles, cutting through the layers to form 18 long strips. Lay out a strip of pastry and brush with oil, then place a heaped teaspoon of mixture into the bottom corner of the filo. Fold the pastry and filling over to create a small triangle to cover the filling. Continue to flip the triangle across the pastry strip until the filling is covered and the pastry is used up. Repeat with the remaining filling and pastry.

Arrange on the baking trays and brush with oil, then bake for 15-20 minutes.

To make the dip, boil the podded broad beans for 5-6 minutes, then drain and rinse with cold water. Place in a food processor with all the other ingredients and blitz, or blend using a hand-held blender. Serve with the warm parcels.

Spaghetti with peas, dill and crème fraîche

This heatwave has outstayed its welcome. The grass is yellow and arid-looking and even I, pale-skinned English rose, have a slight tan. I travel to see my friend Carina in north Wales and sit on a long train journey in 28C heat.

I arrive in Rhyl (sunny Prestatyn, a reminder from my A Level English days, is just down the road), hot and sweaty, and we head to the nearest beer garden. I drink a glass of cold white wine and then another. We head back to the house and I make a very easy spaghetti dish with fresh peas, shelling them as we open another bottle of wine. It soaks up some of the booze, but I inevitably wake the next morning with a slight hangover.

Under 15 minutes | Serves 4

Ingredients

- 250g peas (fresh or frozen)
- 250g spaghetti
- 2 cloves garlic, finely chopped or grated
- 1 tbsp olive oil
- The juice of 1 lemon
- 4-5 handfuls spinach
- 1 tub of vegan crème fraîche, such as Oatly
- Fresh dill, roughly chopped
- Ground black pepper

Bring a large pan of salted water to the boil. Cook the spaghetti for 5 minutes then add the peas and cook for 4 minutes. Meanwhile, fry the garlic in the olive oil until golden and turn off the heat. When cooked, drain the spaghetti and peas (keep a little of the water) and add to the pan with the garlic. Add the spinach then pour over the lemon juice and warm on a low heat for 1-2 minutes, until the spinach has wilted. Turn off the heat and stir through the crème fraîche, add the chopped dill and plenty of black pepper, and serve.

Lemony samphire with almonds

The beautiful weather continues, and after writing at home for most of the day, I'm itching to get outside and feel the warm air on my face. When Kieron gets home, he drives us west to Mumbles. It's a gorgeous evening and we walk along the newly refurbished pier, with Mumbles Lighthouse in the distance, and share a cone of chips. We watch the sun set, a pinky orange stripe on the horizon.

When we get home, it's late and I'm still hungry – it must be the sea air. I fancy something fresh – and quick – to eat, so I stir-fry samphire with almonds and lemon juice. It's a simple supper: salty, zesty and very tasty.

Under 5 minutes | Serves 2

Ingredients

– 1 packet of samphire, rinsed and drained
– A glug of olive or rapeseed oil
– The juice of 1 lemon
– 2 handfuls whole almonds

In a large frying pan, heat the oil over a medium temperature. Add the samphire with the lemon juice and almonds and fry for about 3 minutes. Serve immediately.

Courgette, pea and spinach soup

I've had a sociable weekend. On Friday, I have a rare night out in Cardiff with my friend Verity and we drink gin and eat tapas. On Saturday, I see my school pals for the first time in months. I feel like the old me. Swansea's OK, but life has changed a lot in recent years.

The next day, I feel a bit bleary and I take a long walk in the afternoon sun. Afterwards, I make a fresh and gloriously green soup using new season courgettes and fresh peas. It's ready in the blink of an eyelid – well, almost – and perfect for this balmy summer evening. You could make this in the autumn with frozen peas, as courgettes are around well into September and sometimes October too.

Under 20 minutes | Serves 3-4

Ingredients

- 1 shallot or small onion, peeled and diced
- 1 tbsp coconut oil
- 1 inch fresh ginger, peeled and grated
- 1 large courgette, diced
- 200g fresh or frozen peas
- 500ml vegetable stock
- 3-4 large handfuls spinach
- 1 lime (juice only)
- A pinch of chilli flakes (optional)
- Salt and pepper

Melt the coconut oil over a medium heat and fry the shallots for 2–3 minutes until soft. Add the ginger, chilli flakes and courgettes and cook for another 2–3 minutes. Add the peas, the stock and a little salt and pepper and bring to the boil, then cook for 4 minutes. Add the spinach and lime juice and stir, and cook for 2 minutes until the spinach has wilted. Turn off the heat and use a stick blender to blend.

Roasted broccoli steaks with miso bean mash, roasted tomatoes and salsa verde

This morning I feel somewhat weary after a busy weekend and I take a long walk to get my brain into gear. Work is quiet today, although I have a fair bit of writing to do – but first, lunch. I fancy something nourishing and comforting, and with some time on my hands, I make a fancy meal. These broccoli steaks work very well and I like the taste and texture.

Unusually for me, I retire to the sofa and watch an episode of The Crown, on which I've been busily binging in my free time. It feels indulgent for a workday and afterwards I hide my phone away so that I can spend a couple of hours writing without the distraction of Instagram, my worst enemy at times. It works and I'm pleased.

Under 40 minutes | Serves 2

Ingredients

For the steaks
– 1 small head of broccoli
– 4 tbsp olive oil
– The juice of 1 lemon
– Salt and pepper
– 6-8 cherry tomatoes
– A few sprigs of fresh thyme

For the mash
– 1 x 400g can butterbeans, rinsed
     and drained
– 1 clove garlic, peeled
     and finely chopped
– 2 tbsp olive oil
– The juice of 1 lemon
– 2 tsp miso paste

For the salsa verde
– 2 large handfuls of kale
– 1 small bunch of parsley,
     stalks included
– 3 tbsp olive oil
– 2 tbsp apple cider
     or balsamic vinegar
– 1 clove garlic, peeled
– A pinch of salt
– A little water

Preheat the oven to 200C. Slice across the length of the broccoli to make a thick 'steak'. In a bowl or jar, combine the olive oil, lemon juice and salt and pepper. Put the 'steaks', lying down, in an ovenproof dish and spoon over half the oil mixture. Place on the top shelf of the oven and roast for 15 minutes. Remove the dish from the oven, turn the 'steaks' over and spoon over the rest of the oil. Add the cherry tomatoes and the thyme and return to the oven to roast for another 10 minutes.

Meanwhile, make the mash. Fry the garlic in the olive oil over a low temperature until golden. Add the butter beans, the lemon juice and the miso and stir. After 2 minutes, turn off the heat and set aside.

Quickly make the salsa verde by adding all the ingredients to a blender and blitzing – or place in a bowl and use a hand-held blender.

Remove the dish from the oven and divide the broccoli, tomatoes and crispy thyme onto two plates. Add the cooking juices into the bean mixture and roughly mash using a potato masher, adding more oil or a little oat milk if you'd like a creamier consistency. Serve alongside the broccoli and tomatoes and spoon over the salsa verde.

Smashed cucumber and mint salad

Suddenly it's August, the hottest of all the months. At the beginning of the month, I spend a few days in London for work and play. It's muggy and I walk the streets of Brick Lane, eat vegan junk food and drink wine at hipster bars while I write.

I celebrate my friend Dania's hen party and it's fun, but I'm glad to get home. I look for something to eat and find a cucumber, which is often underrated. It adds crunch to sandwiches and salads, but rarely is it celebrated for its own clean and fresh flavour. I make a simple salad – and this one requires an apron. Smashing the cucumber brings out the flavour and is, unsurprisingly, rather therapeutic.

Under 20 minutes | Serves 3-4 as a side dish

Ingredients

– 1 large cucumber, whole
– 2-3 tbsp rice vinegar
– 5-6 leaves fresh mint, roughly chopped
– 1 tsp sea salt

Using a rolling pin, bash the cucumber until it splits in half. As this can be a bit messy, it's a good idea to wear an apron! Roughly chop the cucumber and place in a large bowl with the other ingredients. Marinade for 10-15 minutes or longer, and serve.

Cucumber gazpacho

My new job starts with a bang — it's busy — and life become more of a juggling act than before. My brain is still a bit addled after my trip away to London (I'm getting too old for two nights' drinking on the trot), but I immediately like my new colleagues and I have a good feeling about the place.

The days are sultry and one evening, feeling tired and jaded after my train back to Swansea is delayed, I enjoy a bowl of cooling cucumber gazpacho, made the night before. It's just the right combination of restorative and rejuvenating and afterwards I head out for a quick stroll before the sun goes down.

15 minutes, plus 2 hours in the fridge | Serves 4-6

Ingredients

- 2–3 cucumbers, cut into chunks
- 1 onion, peeled and diced
- 2 garlic cloves, peeled and crushed
- 1 slice of white bread, roughly torn
- 350ml hot vegetable stock
- 4 tsp rice vinegar
- 1–2 tsp tabasco sauce
- 1 tbsp sugar
- Fresh basil
- Flaked almonds

Blend the cucumber, onion, garlic and bread using a food processor or a hand-held blender. You should end up with a fairly smooth mixture. Tip into a large bowl and pour over the hot stock and the other ingredients and stir. Leave to cool, then when at room temperature, cover and refrigerate for at least two hours.

Serve with toasted flaked almonds and torn basil leaves.

Shakshuka

Finally, it's the weekend, a time to sleep in and switch off. I'm really not a morning person, but I love breakfast, or even better, brunch.

Today, I make shakshuka, the classic Middle Eastern dish, which adorns brunch menus at hipster cafes across the land. The word 'shakshuka' comes from an Arabic verb which means to 'stick or clump together', and as I've never been one to follow rules, I use tofu instead of the usual eggs. With the right seasoning, it works, and packs a protein-filled punch – and it's a great way to cook with seasonal tomatoes and peppers. I have the whole weekend to myself, a rare thing, so I go to the gym, read and cook.

1 hour 10 minutes | Serves 4

Ingredients

For the tofu
− 1 block (400g) firm tofu
− The juice of half a lemon
− 1 tsp ground cumin
− 1 tsp sweet paprika
− 1 tsp ground cinnamon
− Pinch of chilli flakes or powder
− A little plant milk (optional)
− Salt and pepper

For the tomato base
− 4 tbsp olive oil
− 1 onion, peeled and finely sliced
− 1 red pepper, diced
− 1 yellow pepper, diced
− 2 garlic cloves, peeled and crushed
− 1 tsp sweet paprika
− 1 tsp smoked paprika
− 1 tsp cumin powder
− 1 tsp sumac
− 1 tsp cinnamon powder
− 800g tinned tomatoes
        (or ripe tomatoes in season)
− 2 tsp sugar
− The juice of 1 lemon
− Small bunch of fresh parsley,
        roughly chopped

Take the tofu and use kitchen roll or a clean tea towel to blot and absorb all its water. Take two heavy wooden chopping boards and place on either side of the block to 'press' it and absorb excess moisture. If you can, put something heavy, like a hardback book, on top of the chopping board to weigh it down further. Leave for 15-20 minutes then put in a bowl and mash it up with a fork. Add lemon juice, salt and spices, and mash together. Heat the oil in a non-stick pan over a low heat and cook the tofu for 5 minutes, stirring regularly. Stir through a little plant milk if you want a creamier consistency. Once it's brown, it's ready. Transfer to a bowl and set aside.

Using the same pan, heat the oil over a medium temperature and add the onion. Cook until golden, then add the peppers. Fry until both are soft, then stir in the garlic and spices and cook for another couple of minutes. Pour in the tomatoes and roughly mash. Add half a cupful of water, then stir in the sugar and lemon juice, bring to a boil, then turn down the heat and simmer for 30 minutes. Taste and season, adding more spice, if you like.

Make 4–8 wells in the sauce and spoon in the scrambled tofu. Season lightly, turn the heat right down as low as possible, cover and cook for about 10 minutes. Sprinkle with parsley and serve with bread and, if you like, a little coconut yoghurt.

Pea and runner bean pasta with pesto

I wake up tired and grumpy after a less than restful night's sleep. I can be snappy and sullen before coffee and this morning there's no time to make any before heading to the train station. Halfway through the walk, the heavens open. I'm wearing sandals and I get soaked. It's not the best start to the day.

I'm flat and frizzy, and that's just my hair, but I have a productive morning at the office before I schlep off, still soggy, to a meeting. When I get home, I change into my pyjamas and make a one-pot pasta dish using late summer vegetables. I eat it, watching TV, with Bobbie on my lap. She's always a comfort when I'm feeling Eeyore-esque.

Under 20 minutes | Serves 3-4

Ingredients

- 100g peas, fresh or frozen
- 100g runner beans, diagonally sliced
- 200g fusilli or penne pasta
- 1 x 400g can cannellini beans, rinsed and drained
- The juice of 1 lemon
- Salt and pepper

For the pesto

- 50g nuts of your choice
- 4-5 tbsp extra virgin olive oil
- The juice of 1 lemon
- 5-6 basil leaves, torn and stalks removed, plus extra for garnishing
- 5-6 mint leaves torn and stalks removed, plus extra for garnishing
- 2 garlic cloves, peeled and cut finely or grated
- 2 large handfuls spinach
- A dash of plant milk
- Salt and pepper

Place the pasta into a large pan and pour over 500ml boiling water, then add the lemon juice and season. Cover with a lid and bring to the boil. Remove the lid and cook on a high heat for 5 minutes, then add the runner beans and after 2 minutes, add the peas and cook for another 3 minutes. Remove the pan from the heat and drain away any residual water from the pasta and return to the pan.

Meanwhile, quickly make the pesto by placing all the ingredients in a food processor and pulsing on a high setting for a minute or two. Add the cannellini beans to the pan and stir through with the pesto. Scatter over the leftover mint and basil leaves and serve.

Raspberry and tahini blondies

Tomorrow we go to Alton Towers and I bake something for the long car ride there. Like Goldilocks, it has taken me a while to get the recipe for these blondies *just* right (baking for too long and cutting into them when warm results in a too-crumbly texture). The blondie, invented a few years before its more famous cousin, the brownie, reminds me of trips to Arnold's and Diner 77, the American-style diners of old Cardiff.

When we arrive at the theme park, it's raining, but we wear our waterproofs and hop on some rides. I'll never understand the appeal of theme parks, but the monkeys are happy. I sit out most of the rides, but rather enjoy the sedate and child-friendly pirate ship, which is much more suited to my level of adventure.

50 minutes, plus cooling time | Makes 12 blondies

Ingredients

- 200g plain flour
- 1 tsp baking powder
- 1 tsp bicarbonate of soda
- 2 tsp ground cinnamon
- 150g vegan butter or margarine (at room temperature)
- 150g brown sugar
- 2 tbsp plant milk
- 3 tbsp tahini
- 1 tsp vanilla extract
- 250g raspberries
- 50g walnuts, chopped

Preheat the oven to 180C and line an 8-inch brownie tin with greaseproof paper.

Melt the butter in a pan and allow to cool. Sieve the flour, baking soda, bicarbonate of soda and cinnamon into a large bowl and mix together. In another large bowl, beat the melted butter, sugar, milk, tahini and vanilla extract. Slowly beat in the flour mixture, then stir in the raspberries and walnuts until you have a thick batter.

Pour the batter into the lined tin and spread evenly. Bake for 25-30 minutes – you'll know if they're cooked if a baking skewer inserted into the cake comes out clean. Place on a cooling rack and allow to cool for an hour or so before cutting into 12 pieces. Slicing before this will result in very crumbly blondies – though they'll still taste delicious.

These will keep in an airtight container for 2-3 days.

Tomato and corn salad

It's a Sunday morning in late August and I meet a friend for coffee. After she leaves, I pull out my laptop. My work-life balance becomes a bit blurred when I work from home, because it's difficult to work your inner Carrie Bradshaw when a pile of dirty dishes is in view. I drink one too many coffees and go for a quick walk to rid myself of the jitters.

For lunch, I make a sunny salad using sweetcorn from the cob (I love these sweet little golden nuggets) and juicy tomatoes. I make a big bowlful, enough to serve a few people, but as it's just me today, it'll do very well for a few packed lunches during the week.

Under 25 minutes | Makes one large bowl

Ingredients

− 4 corn on the cobs
− 8 large tomatoes
− 4 tbsp sesame oil
− The juice of 1 lime
− A handful fresh parsley
− Salt and pepper

Bring a pan of salted water to the boil then cook the corn on the cob for 10 minutes. Drain and leave to cool. Slice the tomatoes then make the dressing by mixing the sesame oil, lime juice, parsley and salt and pepper together in a bowl or glass.

Using a knife, cut off the corn husks and put into a large bowl. Layer over the sliced tomatoes and then pour over the dressing and serve.

Strawberry and basil sling

I'm always a bit sad when the last bank holiday weekend of the year comes around. I'm a bit swamped with work so I say no to drinks in Cardiff, not fancying the two-hour round trip and the inevitable hangover in the morning. These days, more than three drinks are certain to kill my productivity the next day.

It's a lovely evening, still and warm, and after doing some writing I decide to make myself a drink – it is the bank holiday after all. There are some slightly sad-looking strawberries in the fridge, which I use to make a refreshing drink to enjoy as the sun starts to go down. I'm too lazy to use a cocktail shaker, but you can if you like.

Under 10 minutes | Serves 2

Ingredients

– 8-10 strawberries, hulls removed
– 25g caster sugar
– The juice of half a lemon
– 8 leaves fresh basil
– A handful of crushed ice (or 3-4 ice cubes for each glass)
– 100ml gin
– 300ml soda water

In a blender, blitz the strawberries, sugar and lemon juice (or, in a bowl, mash the strawberries, add the sugar and then stir). Set to one side. Using a pestle and mortar, gently bash the basil leaves (or use a rolling pin) and divide the mixture into two glasses. Fill each glass with ice, then pour over the strawberry mixture followed by the gin. Give it a good stir, then pour over the soda water and serve.

Summer berry and coconut milk ice lollies

It's Bank Holiday Sunday and I wake to daylight streaming through the blinds – and Bobbie clawing at my toes. I have a glut of summer berries to use up and I make ice lollies before we go for a trip to the seaside. I leave them to set in the freezer and slap on some sun cream.

After battered tofish and chips, the monkeys spend some time in the games arcade, while I stroll along Mumbles Pier, soaking up the last of the summer sun. We stop for an ice cream (a vegan Magnum for me) before we head back to the car and I spend the journey feeling slightly sick. Later that evening, still blisteringly hot, I remember the ice lollies and I savour one, dribbling coconut milk down my chin.

10 minutes, plus freezing time | Makes 4 lollies

Ingredients

– 1 x 400ml can full fat coconut milk
– 1 punnet strawberries, hulled and sliced
– 1 punnet raspberries
– 1 handful fresh mint, chopped, stalks removed

In a large bowl, stir together all the ingredients and spoon into ice lolly moulds. Place in the freezer and when frozen, remove from the moulds and enjoy.

Whole roasted fennel with cherries and pistachios and creamy polenta mash

Adios August, month of holidays, half empty offices and the National Eisteddfod. Summer's coming to an end and autumn is in the air, but it's not here just yet. It's still too warm to wear a jumper but the shops are full of winter coats and in just a month or so, there could be a Christmas tree in the window of Marks and Spencer.

I make a meal to see out the last day of the summer. I roast fennel and add creamy polenta mash and a bright red cherry sauce. It's comforting but light enough for the still warm summer weather. Don't be put off by the different components of the meal as this is very easy to put together, although removing the stones from the cherries is a bit fiddly – and messy.

Under 1 hour | Serves 4

Ingredients

– 4 fennel bulbs
– 4 tbsp olive oil
– The juice of 1 orange
– Salt and pepper
– 50g pistachios, shelled
  and roughly chopped

For the polenta mash
– 150g quick-cook polenta
– 600ml boiling water
– 150ml oat milk
– 2 tbsp olive oil
– 2 tbsp maple syrup
– The juice of 1 lemon
– Salt and pepper

For the cherry sauce
– 300g cherries, stones removed
– 50ml water
– 50g white sugar
– 2 tbsp balsamic vinegar
– A pinch of salt

Preheat the oven to 150C. Put the fennel bulbs in a large roasting dish and drizzle over the olive oil and orange juice and season with salt and pepper. Roast for 40-45 minutes or until golden and tender.

While the fennel is cooking, make the cherry sauce. Roughly chop the cherries, discard the stones, and put in a saucepan with the sugar, water, balsamic vinegar and salt, and heat over a low temperature for about 5 minutes.

Quickly make the polenta. Pour the boiling water into a large pan, add a good pinch of salt and heat over a medium temperature. Slowly pour in the polenta, then stir constantly for 4–5 minutes – be careful as it can bubble almost volcanically. When the polenta is firm and begins to come away from the sides of the pan, turn off the heat. Add the oat milk, olive oil, maple syrup and lemon juice and season, then stir well.

Take four plates and spoon a dollop of polenta mash onto each of them. Take the fennel out of the oven and carefully cut in half lengthways. Layer the two halves on top of the mash on each plate and scatter over the pistachios. Divide the cherry sauce between the four plates and serve.

Autumn

Hello autumn, my old friend. I love this time of year with its carpets of copper-coloured leaves and bonfires burning bright, but I also feel a bit undone by it. Just as the changing colours bring me joy, they also make me sad. Autumn can be the most melancholy time of year, a cruel mistress who leads you in with her beauty but eventually leaves you cold. At least I can take solace in her wares.

It's the season for auburn apples, blackberries, plums and sunny squashes.

In season now…

Apples, artichokes, aubergine, beetroot, blackberries, broccoli, butternut squash, carrots, cauliflower, celeriac, celery, chard, chicory, courgettes, cucumber, damsons, elderberries, fennel, garlic, gooseberries, Jerusalem artichokes, kale, kohlrabi, leeks, lettuce, marrow, mushrooms, new potatoes, onions, pak choi, parsnips, pears, plums, pumpkin, radishes, red cabbage, rocket, runner beans, salsify, samphire, shallots, sorrel, squash, swede, sweetcorn, sweet potatoes, sweetcorn, tomatoes, turnips, watercress.

Aubergine with mint, pistachios and olives

I t's September, the start of the school term and back to business as usual, but I'm not ready to see the back of summer just yet – and I feel the same way about eating. In the crossover period between the August bank holiday and early autumn, it'll be a while before we want to hibernate at home with pie and mash. The aubergine (or eggplant in America) is a much misunderstood vegetable, but cook it the right way and you'll be rewarded. Back in the summer, I ate the most wonderful aubergine at Bar 44 – go there for the best tapas in Cardiff – and tonight, I try to replicate it. I roast the aubergines slow and low and the result is deliciously soft and velvety. My tastebuds are in heaven.

Under 1 hour | Serves 4 as a side (or two as a main course)

Ingredients

– 2 aubergines, ends removed
– A generous glug of olive oil
– A good pinch of sea salt

For the chickpeas
– 1 x 400g can chickpeas,
      rinsed and drained
– The juice of 1 lemon
– 2 tbsp extra virgin olive oil
– 2 tsp sumac
– A good pinch of sea salt

For the dressing
– 4 tbsp extra virgin olive oil
– 2 tbsp pomegranate molasses
– The juice of 1 lemon
– 2 tsp sumac
– 1 tsp miso paste
– A good pinch of sea salt

To garnish
– A handful of pistachios, shelled
      and roughly chopped
– 1 x 340g jar green olives, drained
      and sliced in half
– A handful of fresh mint leaves, torn

Preheat the oven to 180C. Place the aubergines in an ovenproof dish, then, using a sharp knife, make small incisions in both. Pour a generous glug of olive oil over both aubergines and sprinkle over some salt and massage. Place on the top shelf of the oven and roast for 40 minutes.

Meanwhile, put the chickpeas in a bowl and add the lemon juice, salt, sumac and olive oil. Leave to marinate. Make your dressing by combining all of the ingredients.

After 40 minutes, remove the aubergines from the oven and pour over the dressing. Return to the oven and roast for a further 5 minutes. Remove from the oven and allow to cool slightly. Divide the chickpeas between four dishes and cut each aubergine lengthways and then lengthways again so that you have eight slices. In each bowl, arrange two slices on top of the chickpeas, then scatter over the pistachios, mint and olives and drizzle over a little tahini, and serve.

Autumn fruits smoothie

The sun is still shining, but the leaves are already falling and plump blackberries are sitting on the hedges, waiting to be eaten. As a city dweller, I've come to blackberry picking late in life, but it's been something of a revelation. I've started to notice other 'pickers' on my walks, and we smile at each other. It's a bit like being in a secret club: if you know, you know. Having said that, blackberry picking is one of the most accessible activities; just remember to be careful of thorns and wash the berries thoroughly. If you end up with too much, you can freeze them for eating another time.

On Monday morning, I make a simple smoothie – an abundance of autumn fruits – which I drink, rather unromantically, on the train to the office.

Under 5 minutes | Serves 2

Ingredients

– 250g blackberries
– 2 plums, destoned
– 1 apple, core removed
      and cut into quarters
– 400ml oat milk
– 1 tsp cinnamon
– 2 heaped tbsp peanut butter

Simply put all the ingredients into a food processor, blitz for a minute until smooth, and pour into two glasses.

Hoisin pulled jackfruit with cashew fried rice and plum sauce

When my plate gets too full (as it sometimes does in more ways than one), I find that fresh air helps to stop the whirring thoughts inside my head. It's a sunny Sunday morning and we walk up Kilvey Hill, somewhere we occasionally go to stretch our legs and look down on Swansea.

I'm still thinking about last night's dinner. I made a Chinese 'fakeaway' with jackfruit, the most delicious hoisin coating and a vividly purple sauce to use up the last of the autumn plums. Sadly there are no leftovers, but I have frozen some of the plum sauce so that I can make the dish again. After the walk, I feel ten times better and decide that work can wait while I read the Sunday papers, a rare treat indeed.

Under 40 minutes | Serves 2

Ingredients

For the jackfruit
– 1 x 482g can jackfruit pieces, drained
– 2 tbsp sesame oil
– 3 tbsp soy sauce
– 1 clove garlic, peeled and minced
– 2 tbsp brown sugar
– 50ml water
– ½ green chilli, sliced
– The juice of half a lime
– 1 tbsp cornflour

For the plum sauce
– 6 plums (about 100g), destoned and cut into small chunks
– 2 tsp Chinese five spice
– 1 tsp salt
– 2 tbsp white rice vinegar
– 2 tbsp brown sugar
– 50ml water

For the rice
– 1 tbsp sesame oil
– 50g cashews
– 120g brown rice, rinsed and drained
– The juice of half a lime

Rinse and drain the rice and add to a pan of cold water. Bring to the boil and cook for 20 minutes then drain and set aside.

Meanwhile, prepare the jackfruit by cutting into thin strips using a sharp knife (keep the edible stems and seeds), then in a large pan over a medium heat, add the sesame oil, soy sauce and garlic and fry for 2-3 minutes. Add the shredded jackfruit with the chilli, brown sugar and half the water and fry for 20 minutes. Halfway through, add the cornflour and the rest of the water and stir every so often.

Make the plum sauce by adding all the ingredients to a saucepan and cooking over a low heat for 10 minutes.

In a large pan or wok, heat the sesame oil and add the cashews, rice and cashews and fry for ten minutes.

When everything is ready, divide between two plates and enjoy. This is nice served with green vegetables.

Fennel, butterbean and black olive stew with orzo

It's late September and while it's still sunny, I'm going bare-legged. Life has been busy and I haven't had time to cook (or clean the hob) so takeaways and ready meals have become a regular occurrence. It's time to eat a bit more healthily, so thank goodness for easy one pot meals that simmer away in the background while I work. As I write, Bobbie often walks over my laptop, typing random letters and numbers on the page, which is particularly unhelpful when I'm proofreading.

At least there's always stew. It's warm and comforting and the longer you leave it to cook, the richer it gets – like any great love affair. This one is healthy but feels rather grown up and glamorous and begs to be enjoyed with a large glass of red, which I happily do.

Under 35 minutes | Serves 3-4

Ingredients

– 4-5 celery stalks, chopped
– 1 large fennel bulb, roughly sliced
    (keep the fronds and roughly chop)
– 150g orzo
– 1 x 400g can tomatoes (chopped or plum)
    plus a can of water
– 2 tsp tomato purée
– 1/2 a 330g jar of pitted black olives, plus a little brine
– 1 x 400g can butterbeans, drained
– 1 tbsp olive oil
– 2 tbsp balsamic vinegar
– Salt and pepper

Over a medium heat, warm the olive oil and fry the celery for 2-3 minutes. Add the fennel (keep the fronds for later) and cook for another 5 minutes. Add the tomatoes, the water and the tomato purée and season. Bring to the boil, then lower the heat and cover with a lid. Leave to simmer for 10 minutes then remove the lid and add the orzo and butterbeans. Bring to the boil and cook for 5-6 minutes, stirring frequently. Add the olives and brine and cook for another minute. Stir through the chopped fennel fronds and serve.

Smoky squash houmous

I'm a big scaredy cat and can barely watch five minutes of a horror film before running behind the sofa – and the only thing I like about Halloween is the pumpkins. That's a little while off, but gorgeous gourds are already piled high at my local greengrocers.

I love to cook with pumpkin and squash, and tonight make a smoky squash houmous, using my secret ingredient: maple syrup. I make a big batch and smear it on toast for a couple of days.

1 hour | Makes one big bowlful

Ingredients

– 200g squash, peeled and deseeded and chopped into small pieces
– 1 tbsp olive oil
– 5-6 sage leaves, or 2 tsp dried
– 1 x 400g can chickpeas, rinsed and drained
– 2 tbsp tahini
– 3 tbsp olive oil
– 1 tsp ground allspice
– A pinch of chilli flakes
– 1 tbsp maple syrup
– 1 clove garlic, peeled
– Salt and pepper, to season

Preheat the oven to 200C. Slice the pumpkin or squash into wedges, place in an ovenproof dish and drizzle with oil, then add the sage leaves. Cook for about 35-40 minutes, and once cooled, place in a blender with the chickpeas, garlic, tahini, allspice, chilli flakes, olive oil and maple syrup, and blend. Add a tablespoon of water if you think it's too thick but it should have quite a chunky texture. Season with salt and pepper and serve on toast, baked potatoes or with salad.

Autumnal salad with kale, walnuts and blackberries

We haven't heard the last swansong of summer just yet, but there's definitely a chill in the air. This week, I've worn a jumper for the first time in months, and I have been almost tempted to put the heating on. The nights may be drawing in, but it's not quite the weather for comfort food; it's the 'season of mists and mellow fruitfulness', with root vegetables, blackberries, apples and plump plums.

My work–life balance isn't too healthy at the moment and I can't be bothered to cook, so I make a simple, seasonal salad for this in-between summer and autumn weather. It's a lovely way to make the most of blackberry season and if you don't have time to go picking, or don't live close to where they grow, just buy them from the supermarket or greengrocer.

Under 20 minutes | Serves 3-4

Ingredients

- 1 x 180g bag pre-cut kale (or buy the
    leaves and roughly chop),
    rinsed and drained
- The juice of 2 lemons
- 4 tbsp extra virgin olive oil
- A generous pinch of sea salt
- 2 parsnips, peeled and grated
- 2 small apples, cored and thinly sliced
- 1 x 400g can chickpeas, rinsed
    and drained
- 100g blackberries
- 100g walnuts

For the blackberry vinaigrette
- 100g blackberries
- 1 tbsp extra virgin olive oil
- 1 tbsp balsamic or
    apple cider vinegar
- 1 tbsp caster sugar
- A generous pinch of sea salt

Put the kale in a large bowl and add 3 tbsp olive oil, the juice of 1 lemon and some salt. Using your hands, massage the kale until each leaf is covered in the mixture. Add the grated parsnip, the sliced apple and the chickpeas, then cover with 1 tbsp olive oil, the rest of the lemon juice and a little more salt. Massage again to combine all the ingredients. Scatter over the blackberries and walnuts.

Quickly make the vinaigrette by placing all the ingredients in a bowl and blending using a hand-held mixer (or put them in a food processor or blender). Serve the salad and drizzle over the vinaigrette.

Roasted celeriac steaks with a blackberry jus and mashed swede

It's grey and gloomy in Swansea and I'm struggling to do everything that I feel I should be doing. We're heading to London this weekend for my friend Dania's wedding and I know that celebrating her special day and seeing university friends will lift my spirits, but right now, I want to lie in bed and read all day.

I get up and force myself to go for a short run, and feeling better afterwards, I manage a couple of hours' work. After lunch, the dark skies break into a smile of sunshine and I take the opportunity to go for a walk, which gives me some thinking time. I feel brighter by the end of the day and make a special meal, which is both comforting and restorative, and I feel more like 'me' again.

1 hour | Serves 4

Ingredients

For the steaks

– 1 large celeriac, peeled and knobbly ends removed
– 2 tbsp olive oil
– 2 tsp wholegrain mustard
– 2 tbsp apple cider vinegar
– 2 tbsp brown sugar

For the jus
– 150g blackberries, washed and drained
– 2 tbsp balsamic vinegar
– 2 tbsp caster sugar
– A little water

For the swede mash
– 2 swedes, peeled and cut into chunks
– 3 tbsp olive oil or vegan butter
– A little oat milk
– Salt and pepper

Preheat the oven to 200C. Holding the celeriac lengthways, slice four disc-like slices (they should be fairly thick). Place in a large ovenproof dish with plenty of room for each slice. Make the marinade by mixing together the oil, mustard, vinegar and sugar. Use half to coat the top end of each slice. Roast for about an hour. Halfway through cooking, remove from the oven, turn over and coat the other side of the steaks with the remainder of the marinade.

Meanwhile, make the mash. Bring a pan of salted water to the boil and cook the swede for about 25–30 minutes until tender. Drain, add the oil or butter, the oat milk and the salt and pepper and mash using a potato masher.

To make the jus, simply add all the ingredients to a large pan and heat over a low heat for 5 minutes.

When the celeriac steaks are cooked, divide onto plates and drizzle over the jus. Serve with the mashed swede.

Apple and pear crumble with vanilla custard

I agree with A. E. Housman, who once wrote 'I love no leafless land', but I have a love-hate relationship with autumn. I love crunchy russet leaves and misty skies, but not so much the darkness and the cold. Now that the clocks have gone back, it gets dark at 5pm and I hate being less able to go outside and roam free.

Still, it's a good opportunity to eat comfort food. Today, hormonal and hungover from two glasses of wine last night (I should have stopped at one), I'm craving a cwtch in carbohydrate form, so I rustle up a crumble using apples and juicy pears. I also make thick yellow custard which I pour over the crumble with wild abandon.

1 hour 10 minutes | Serves 4-6

Ingredients

- 300g apples (3 medium apples), cored and sliced into small chunks
- 250g pears (3 medium pears), cored and sliced into small chunks
- 2 tsp cinnamon
- 1 tsp ground allspice
- 1 tsp vanilla extract
- 150ml water

For the crumble
- 250g plain flour
- 150g caster sugar
- 160g cold vegan butter or margarine

For the custard
- 500 ml oat milk
- 100g white sugar
- 2 tsp vanilla extract
- A pinch of sea salt
- 1 tbsp cornflour
- A pinch of turmeric (optional)

Preheat the oven to 190C. Put the apples in a saucepan with the water, spices and vanilla extract and heat over a low temperature for 5 minutes. Add the pears and heat for another 5 minutes, then set aside. Put in a large baking dish (I use a 10 x 8 inch dish) and flatten down with a large spoon to prevent too much crumble falling through.

Put the flour and sugar in a bowl, then add the cold butter or margarine and rub it in with your fingertips until the mixture looks like moist breadcrumbs. Pour the crumb mix over the fruit to form a pile in the centre, then use a fork to even out.

Place in the preheated oven for 35-40 minutes, until the top is golden.

Meanwhile, make the custard. Put the oat milk, vanilla, salt and sugar in a small saucepan and heat over a medium heat, stirring constantly. Add the cornflour and bring to the boil. Keep stirring until you have a thick consistency, then add the turmeric, if using.

When the crumble is cooked, remove from the oven, cut into slices and serve in bowls with the custard poured over.

Pear, courgette and cardamom loaf

It's a miserable Monday morning, and after working at the weekend, I take the day off. I bake a cake, not always the most relaxing thing to do when Bobbie jumps up on the kitchen counters, forever in search of food, even though there's plenty in her bowl.

We're on the cusp of courgette season and pears have been at the greengrocers for a few weeks, so I decide to put the two together. In this cake, the sweetness of the pears and the mild mellowness of the courgettes are lifted by a gentle kick of cardamom. A friend at work can't eat gluten so I use rice flour, but any kind will work. A slice of cake goes very well with a mug of tea and five minutes' peace from Bobbie's meowing.

1 hour, plus cooling time | Makes 1 medium-sized loaf

Ingredients

- 200g rice flour
- 2 tsp baking powder
- 100g porridge oats
- 2 large ripe pears (300g), cored and cubed
- 2 small courgettes (200g), grated
- 100ml vegetable, olive, sunflower or coconut oil
        (plus a little bit extra for greasing the loaf tin)
- 200ml plant milk
- 100g brown sugar
- 1 tsp cinnamon
- 1–2 tsp apple cider vinegar (optional)
- Cardamom (seeds from 5-6 pods)

Preheat the oven to 200C. In a large bowl, sieve over the flour and baking powder and mix together. Add the other ingredients and stir thoroughly. Grease a 9×5-inch loaf tin, add the cake mixture and place on the middle shelf of the oven. Bake for 45-50 minutes or until golden brown and a skewer inserted into the middle of the cake comes out clean. Allow to cool, then serve in slices, perhaps with some coconut yogurt or vegan ice cream.

Pulled mushroom sandwich
with sage aioli

It's October and we're moving into autumn's abyss. After sun-dappled days and crisp evenings, the rain has set in. It's been a week of grey skies, damp leaves and darkness, and the clocks haven't even gone back yet. Still, I'm quite sure that October sunsets are the prettiest and every time their blush spreads across the sky, I smile hoping that tomorrow will be clear and bright.

Today, I work from bed, which is rather nice as I listen to the rain outside pelting on the windows. That evening, I watch two Nora Ephron films back to back. When I hunker down, I hanker for something stodgy and satisfying to eat. I turn to this meaty sandwich, because on these drab days, I need all the vitamin D I can get to improve my mood. I'm not brave enough to pick my own mushrooms – and none grow near me – and I wouldn't recommend it without expert advice.

Under 30 minutes | Serves 2

Ingredients

– 2 tbsp oil
– 4 large mushrooms,
    roughly shredded (250g)
– 1 tbsp maple syrup
– 100ml water
– 1 tsp Marmite
– ½ tsp paprika
– ½ tsp cinnamon
– 4 slices sourdough bread

For the sage aioli
– 100g cashews
– 50ml water
– 5-6 sage leaves
– Pinch of sea salt
– The juice of half a lemon
– 2 gloves garlic, peeled

Heat 1 tbsp oil in a frying pan over a medium heat and fry the sage leaves until crispy. Remove from the pan and set aside. Add another 1 tbsp oil to the pan and fry the shredded mushroom for 2-3 minutes, then add the water, Marmite, cinnamon, smoked paprika and maple syrup. Cook over a low heat for 10-15 minutes.

To make the aioli, simply blend the fried sage with the other ingredients using a hand-held blender or food processor. Spread onto the slices of bread and divide the mushrooms between the two sandwiches.

Pumpkin, lentil and spinach curry with coconut milk and cardamom

On this Thursday afternoon, I sneak off to the cinema where I watch a matinee performance of the new Judy Garland biopic. I leave the screening sad and wet-eyed – and like a pathetic fallacy, it's raining. I dash to the supermarket across the road to stay dry where I pick up a couple of pumpkins, the kings of the cucurbita family and the real symbol of Halloween.

I always think it a shame when jeering jack o'lanterns are thrown away, flesh and all. It's such a waste. I make a warming curry, which once the chopping and peeling is done, is pretty easy to make. It certainly brightens up this damp squib of an evening.

Under 45 minutes | Serves 3-4

Ingredients

– 1 medium (around 600g) pumpkin or squash,
       peeled, diced and seeds removed
– 200g red lentils, rinsed and drained
– 2 x 400ml cans coconut milk
– 1 bag (about 250g), fresh spinach (or use frozen)
– 1 onion, peeled and finely diced
– 1 heaped teaspoon coconut oil
– 1 tsp ground turmeric
– 1 tsp cinnamon
– 2 tsp cumin
– 2 tsp coriander seeds, ground
– 1 tsp cardamom seeds, ground
– 2 inches of ginger, peeled and finely chopped or grated
– 2 cloves of garlic, peeled and finely chopped or grated

Prepare the pumpkin, then in a large pot or saucepan, heat the oil over a low temperature, add the onion, garlic, ginger and spices and fry for 2 minutes. Add the pumpkin and cook for another 5 minutes. Pour in the coconut milk with the lentils and bring to the boil.

Reduce the heat, cover with a lid and simmer for 20 minutes, stirring occasionally. Add the spinach, stir through, and cook for another 2 minutes – or a bit longer if using frozen. Serve with brown rice.

Stuffed squash with lentils, turnip purée and kale salsa verde

It's Kieron's birthday and this morning, before he heads to the Plaid Cymru autumn conference for work, we take a walk to Clyne. At the top of the hill, with Swansea beach in the distance, he gets down on one knee and asks me to marry him – and I say yes.

That night, the three of us celebrate at a chain Italian restaurant, but the next evening I make a special dinner inspired by a meal we enjoyed at a restaurant in Hay when we visited for our anniversary last year. I roast a mini pumpkin, as larger ones are best left for carving into jack-o-lanterns, and it's delicious. Pumpkins can be a real bugger to cut, so be careful.

50 minutes | Serves 2

Ingredients

For the squash
– 1 small squash or pumpkin
– 3 tbsp olive oil
– A generous pinch of salt
– A generous pinch of chilli flakes
– 1 tsp fresh thyme leaves (or use dried)

For the lentil filling
– 75g green lentils, rinsed and drained
– 2 tbsp olive oil
– 1 small shallot, peeled and diced
– 1 garlic clove, peeled and crushed
– 30g dates, chopped
– 3-4 sundried tomatoes, chopped
– A handful of fresh parsley
– The juice of half a lemon
– ½ tsp cinnamon
– Salt and pepper

For the turnip purée
– 1 large turnip (about 200g)
– 50ml oat milk
– 1 tsp brown sugar
– Salt and pepper
– 1 tsp cinnamon
– A grating of fresh nutmeg
　　　(or ½ tsp dried)

For the kale salsa verde
– 2 large handfuls of kale
– 1 handful of parsley
– The juice of half a lemon
– Salt and pepper
– ½ tsp chilli flakes
– 2 tbsp olive oil
– 1 tbsp brown sugar
– 2 sundried tomatoes
– 50 ml water

Preheat the oven to 200C. Holding the squash widthways on a chopping board, use a sharp knife to carefully cut it in half. Scoop out the flesh and seeds and set aside. Place the two squash halves in a roasting dish, facing upwards and drizzle the oil over the two cavities. Add the salt, chilli flakes and thyme, then turn over in the dish. Place on the top shelf of the oven and roast for 35-40 minutes.

If you want to use the leftover pumpkin seeds, remove as much flesh as possible, rinse and drain in a colander and then dry with a clean tea towel. Place in a bowl with 1 tbsp olive oil and a little salt and pepper and mix together. In the last 10 minutes of cooking time, remove the squash from the oven, lay out the seeds across the base of the dish and return to the oven.

While the squash is cooking, make your lentil mixture. Bring a pan of salted water to the boil and cook the lentils for 25 minutes. Meanwhile, boil another pan of salted water, cut the turnip into chunks and boil for 20-25 minutes. When it's ready, turn off the heat and leave in the boiling water.

While the lentils are cooking, take a frying pan, add 1 tbsp olive oil and fry the shallot and garlic over a medium heat for 2-3 minutes, until translucent. Add the drained lentils and all the other ingredients, plus 1 tbsp olive oil, and warm for another 5 minutes or so. Turn off the heat and set aside.

When the squash is ready, remove the dish from the oven, but don't switch it off. Allow the squash to cool for a few minutes, then turn them over and spoon the lentil mixture into both cavities – be generous with your filling. Return to the oven and roast for another 10 minutes.

Quickly make your salsa verde by placing all the ingredients in a large bowl and blitzing with a stick blender – or use a food processor. Set to one side. Now drain the turnip and add to a large bowl with the other ingredients and blitz.

Remove the squash from the oven and get two plates. Spread a layer of turnip purée in the middle of each plate then place the squash half on top. Sprinkle over some of the roasted pumpkin seeds (if using), add a dollop of the salsa verde and serve.

Creamy mushroom soup

One wet Wednesday morning, I head to Cardiff for work. I've muddled up the train times and, in less of a rush than usual, I take the scenic route. It's the crossover period between autumn and winter, and as I walk, I see that summer has gone to seed – but in the most spectacular way. I pass fuzzy orange trees, plucked like turkeys at Christmas, and yellowing hedgerows, slowly dying. The trees are a blaze of colour which contrast with the overcast sky and the industrial estate and new build homes built on the old copperworks in Landore.

The ends of my hair are damp from the rain and when I reach the station, I'm sodden. Tonight I'll make a creamy mushroom soup and thinking about it gets me through a long day at the office.

Under 45 minutes | Serves 4

Ingredients

– 500g mushrooms
– 1 onion, peeled and finely chopped
– 2 cloves of garlic, peeled and crushed
– A few sprigs of fresh flat-leaf parsley
– A few sprigs of fresh thyme, leaves only
– A glug of olive oil
– 1 litre vegetable stock
– 150ml oat milk
– The juice of 1 lemon
– 1 tsp dried thyme
– Half tsp chilli flakes

Wipe the mushrooms with some kitchen roll then finely slice. Heat a splash of olive oil in a large saucepan over a medium heat, add the onion, garlic, parsley stalks, thyme leaves and mushrooms, pop the lid on and cook gently for 7-8 minutes or until softened. Spoon out 2 tablespoons of mushrooms, and keep for later.

Pour the stock into the pan and bring to the boil over a medium heat, turn the heat down to low and simmer for 15 minutes. Season to taste with sea salt and black pepper, pour over the lemon juice and add the dried thyme and chilli flakes, then whizz with a stick blender until smooth.

Pour in the oat milk, stir and spoon the soup into bowls and garnish with the chopped parsley and remaining mushrooms. Serve with crusty bread.

Beetroot ketchup

I see the fifth of November as the first sign that Christmas is on the way. I think back to childhood and all the bright lights, sights and smells: the fires, the screeching Catherine Wheels, the mittened hands clutching sparklers, and of course, the toffee apples, often hard enough to chip a tooth.

I love the smoke and sparkle of Bonfire Night, but these days, I stay in with Bobbie, who is understandably afraid of the bangs and screeches outside. I make baked potatoes and vegan hot dogs, which I smother with my homemade beetroot ketchup. Its vibrant hue almost competes with the fireworks in the sky but the bottle will last for much longer – and it packs a punch in the flavour department.

1 hour 30 minutes | Makes one large jar or bottle

Ingredients

- 2-3 beetroot (about 400g), peeled or
        scrubbed and cut into cubes
- 2 tbsp olive oil
- 1 onion, peeled and diced
- 1 large carrot, peeled and diced
- 2 celery stalks, diced
- 2 garlic cloves, peeled and crushed
- 6 tbsp brown sugar
- 4 tbsp rice vinegar
- 2 tsp sea salt
- 2 tsp smoked paprika
- ½ tsp ground ginger
- ½ tsp ground cinnamon
- Freshly ground pepper

Preheat the oven to 200C. Prepare the beetroot, place in an ovenproof dish and drizzle with olive oil and salt and pepper. Roast for 1.5 hours.

Meanwhile, in a large pan, warm a little olive oil over a low heat and sweat down the onion, garlic, carrot and celery. This will take about 10-15 minutes. When the beetroot is ready, add to the pan with the spices, sugar, salt and vinegar. Cook for another five minutes then remove from the heat. Allow to cool then use a stick blender or food processor to blitz into a smooth paste. Transfer to a sterilised jar or bottle (you'll need a funnel if doing this) and keep for up to two weeks in the fridge.

Roasted cauliflower, tahini and bean soup

Although I will eventually come to dread the quickening approach of night time, I do enjoy, after a crisp but dry autumn day, the sky at dusk. Often rushing from office to train, I don't always see the sun setting or sometimes the pink-streaked shepherd's delight, but I like the way the sharp air feels against my face. Here are people, like me, making the most of the minutes before daylight descends into darkness.

Now that the temperature has dropped, I'm making a lot of soup. This one with roasted cauliflower and tahini is smooth and sultry and quite delicious on a dull and drizzly evening. It's so good that I go back for seconds and I even lick the ladle.

Under 1 hour | Serves 4

Ingredients

- 1 large cauliflower, cut into florets
- 2-3 shallots, skin on
- 3-4 garlic cloves, skin on
- The juice of two lemons
- Salt and pepper
- 1-2 cans white beans
- 1 litre stock
- A generous grating of nutmeg
- 1 tsp sumac
- A pinch of chilli flakes
- 2 tsp fresh or dried thyme
- 2-3 tbsp tahini

Preheat the oven to 200C. Place the cauliflower florets into a large oven dish with the oil and the salt and pepper. Add the shallots and garlic and roast for 30 minutes. Remove from the oven and set aside to cool. When cool, remove the skin from the shallots and garlic.

In a deep pan, heat some oil and add the cauliflower, beans (no need to drain), shallots, and garlic with the lemon juice, the thyme and the spices. Let them brown for a couple of minutes, then pour in the stock and bring to the boil. Simmer for 5 minutes, allow to cool slightly and add the tahini just before blending. Serve with crusty bread.

Jump for joy salad - Romanesco cauliflower and russet apples

Autumn's colours are out and proud and it's a sight to behold. Golden trees, ravishing red leaves and misty skies. After the rain, everything is brighter, more vivid. I'm making the most of it before winter sets in

Last night I sat on the beach and watched the sunset. I really should do it more often. Earlier in the afternoon, I'd popped into Swansea market where I picked up some seasonal treats. Let me introduce you to autumn's finest: sweet but mellow russet apples, ravishing Romanesco cauliflower, and my favourite, the humble sprout. I make a salad to celebrate autumn in all its glory. The sumac in this adds a hint of zesty heat but use ground cumin if you don't have any. Using tinned lentils makes this a really quick and easy dish, but you can, of course, boil dried ones if you prefer.

Under 20 minutes | Serves 2

Ingredients

For the salad
- 1 head of Romanesco cauliflower,
    broken into small florets
    (keep the leaves for cooking,
    so roughly chop these, too)
- 12 sprouts, ends and outer leaves removed
    and chopped finely
- 4 large handfuls of kale or spinach,
    roughly chopped
- 1 russet apple, cut into thin slices
- 1 x 400g can brown or green lentils,
    rinsed and drained
- 2 large handfuls of parsley, chopped
- The juice of half a lemon
- Salt and pepper

For the dressing
- 1 ½ tsp sumac
- 2 tbsp extra virgin olive oil
- 1 tbsp white wine vinegar

Put the cauliflower, sprouts and kale in a large bowl then mix the ingredients for the dressing in a glass or jar. Pour over the vegetables and massage with your hands, then season with salt and pepper.

Heat a large frying pan or wok over a high heat, then stir fry the vegetables for 3-4 minutes, stirring frequently. Add the lentils and cook for another minute. Remove the pan from the heat and tip everything back into the bowl. Add the apple and parsley and stir though, squeeze over the lemon, then serve.

Roasted Jerusalem artichoke and lemon soup

I t's late November and one evening, as I travel back from London by train, I watch the sunset in the sky, a smear of pink stretching across the inky blue sky. It's just gone four in the afternoon and I look forward to winter solstice, less than a month away. The shortest day of the year is a happy sign that the hours of daylight will slowly but surely increase.

The travelling has tired me out, so when I get home I make a reviving soup using some Jerusalem artichokes, which aren't really artichokes at all, but a type of sunflower. I roast them, adding lemon juice for a bit of zing, and blend them into a light and glossy soup.

1 hour 30 minutes | Serves 2

Ingredients

– 400-500g Jerusalem artichokes, peeled and roughly sliced
– 2 unwaxed lemons
– 1 medium onion, peeled and finely diced
– 500ml hot vegetable stock
– Salt and pepper
– Fresh basil leaves, roughly torn
– Olive oil

Preheat the oven to 200C. Put the sliced artichokes into a large oven dish and pour over a generous glug of olive oil. Squeeze the juice from the lemon over them, then add the halves to the dish, and season. Place the dish on the top shelf of the oven and roast for about 45-50 minutes.

When cooked, remove from the oven and set aside. Heat some oil in a large pan and fry the onion for 5 minutes. Pour in the roasted artichokes and lemons (use a little boiling water to loosen the juices from the dish and use these as well) and cook for another 5 minutes. Pour over the hot stock, season, and bring to the boil. Reduce to a simmer, cover with a lid and then cook for another 10 minutes. Turn off the heat, remove the lemon halves from the pan and add the basil leaves, then blend with a hand blender. Serve with bread and a drizzle of extra virgin olive oil.

Spiced parsnip and apple cake

I t's rained for what seems like an entire month and it shows no sign of stopping. On a day like this, I'll usually force myself out for a walk (or sometimes a run), then soggy but sustained by fresh air, I'll come home to dry off and think about making something comforting to eat.

Today I feel like baking, and as parsnips are plentiful at the moment, I add them to this subtly spiced cake. Parsnips are naturally sweet − in fact, they become sweeter during a frost, when some of the starch is converted to sugar − and were used in jams and cakes before sugar was widely available. They're also full of vitamins and fibre, making this bake a little more wholesome than others.

1 hour | Serves 6-8

Ingredients

− 50ml oil, plus extra for greasing
− 100ml plant milk
− 230g self-raising flour
− 1 tsp baking powder
− 1½ tsp ground cinnamon
− 1 tsp allspice
− ½ tsp ground ginger
− ½ tsp nutmeg
− 200g light brown muscovado sugar
− 300g parsnips, coarsely grated
− 1 large apple, coarsely grated

For the icing
− 100g vegan margarine, softened
− 4 tbsp maple syrup
− 50g walnuts

Preheat the oven to 180°C. Grease a 9-inch spring-form cake tin and line the base with baking paper. Sift the flour, baking powder and spices into a large bowl. Add the sugar and grated parsnip and apple, then stir until well combined. Stir in the oil, then mix well.

Pour into the prepared cake tin and bake in the oven for 40-45 minutes or until a skewer comes out clean. Transfer to a cooling rack, leave in the tins for 5 minutes, then turn out and leave to cool completely before icing.

To make the icing, simply blitz the margarine, walnuts and maple syrup using a hand-held blender, then spread evenly on top of the cake.

To store, keep in a cake tin in the fridge for 2-3 days.

Winter

After autumn comes winter, a dark and foreboding month for many. In days of yore, people hibernated, and as we approach winter solstice, the days are short and Christmas can leave us feeling weary. I wake up to dark skies and watch the sun rise, an orange orb in the sky, as I walk to work. On the train to Cardiff, I see frost-covered fields from the window.

It's the season for chestnuts, celeriac, and my favourite, Brussels sprouts.

In season now…

Apples, beetroot, Brussels sprouts, blood oranges★, broccoli, carrots, cauliflower, celeriac, celery, chard, chestnuts, chicory, Jerusalem artichokes, kale, leeks, mushrooms, onions, parsnips, pears, pineapple★, pomegranates★, potatoes, pumpkin, purple sprouting broccoli, radicchio, red cabbage, rhubarb, salsify, satsumas★, Savoy cabbage, shallots, squash, swede, turnips.

★imported

Winter cocktail

So here is December and all its expectant joy. It's dark and bleak outside, but the bright lights of yuletide are here until the last box of mince pies is eaten.

It's a crisp winter Wednesday and a misty morning has made way for piercing blue skies. I get home from work and fancy a short, sharp reviver to celebrate the halfway point until the weekend. I'm not saying that the lead up to Christmas is stressful – or that you need a drink to get through it – but a little festive tipple always goes down well. I turn to tequila, a throwback from my student days, which I now sip rather than slurp. A tot of tonic water and a hint of citrus turns this into a rather sophisticated party drink which can be enjoyed throughout the festive season.

Under 5 minutes | Serves 2

Ingredients

– 100ml white tequila
– 300ml tonic water
– Half an orange
– Sea salt
– 2 tbsp pomegranate seeds

Pour the salt onto a plate or saucer, take two glasses and rub the orange half around the rim of each glass so that they are lightly coated in juice. Place the rim of each glass in the salt and gently turn until the rim is coated. Pour 50ml tequila in each glass, followed by a generous squeeze of orange juice and then add 150ml tonic water to each glass. Remove the pomegranate seeds (place half a pomegranate face down in a bowl and bash with a rolling pin or gently remove with a spoon, making sure to discard the white pith), and add 1tbsp seeds to each glass. Enjoy!

Sticky toffee apple pudding with vanilla custard

Late one Sunday afternoon, I head out for a walk. The sun is low, sneaking out in slivers of silver light and the pale, milky blue sky battles against the grey clouds. I listen to Chet Baker as I walk, his melancholic melody matching the dead, brown leaves on the floor. Skeleton trees sway in the wind.

It starts to rain and the wind against my face feels like hundreds of tiny pins pricking my skin. It's an evening for comfort and indulgence so I make a sticky toffee pudding using dates and apples that have been sitting in the fruit bowl for some time. The end result is gorgeously gooey, and topped with hot custard, it's almost enough to make me forget that it's blowing a gale outside.

1 hour 30 minutes | Serves 8

Ingredients

For the pudding
- 250g dates
- 100g soft brown sugar
- 100g vegan butter,
      plus extra for greasing
- 3 apples, grated
- 300g self-raising flour
- 2 tsp baking powder
- 2 tsp ground allspice
- A pinch of sea salt
- 1 tsp vanilla extract
- 1 tbsp treacle

For the sauce
- 150g vegan butter, softened
- 350g dark muscovado sugar
- 1 tbsp black treacle
- 50ml oat milk
- 1 tsp vanilla extract
- A pinch of sea salt

For the custard
- 1 litre oat milk
- 150g white sugar
- 2 tsp vanilla extract
- A pinch of sea salt
- 1 tbsp cornflour
- A pinch of turmeric (optional)

Preheat the oven to 180C. Put the dates in a bowl and pour over 250ml boiling water and leave for 10 minutes.

In a large bowl, cream the butter and sugar together. Tip in the flour, baking powder, grated apple, allspice and salt and stir well. Add the vanilla extract and treacle and stir again.

Lightly grease a large dish or tin and pour the batter in, making sure to spread evenly. Bake for 30–35 minutes, or until a cake tester comes out clean.

Meanwhile, make the sauce by melting the butter, muscovado sugar and treacle over a very low heat in a heavy-based saucepan. Once the butter is melted, stir gently until everything else is melted too. Now stir in the oat milk, vanilla extract and salt, then turn up the heat and when it's bubbling and hot, take it off the heat.

Take the pudding out of the oven and leave to stand for 20–30 minutes. To make the custard, put the oat milk, vanilla, salt and sugar in a small saucepan and heat over a medium heat, stirring constantly. Add the cornflour and bring to the boil. Keep stirring until you have a thick consistency, then add the turmeric, if using.

Pour the toffee sauce over the pudding and cut into eight slices. Pour over the custard and serve.

Celeriac and white bean dip

We don't go out much these days, but this evening we have friends coming over for drinks and nibbles. I make a creamy dip using half a celeriac that's been hanging around in the fridge. It goes down a treat and it'll be tasty on toast, sandwiches and jacket potatoes, too.

With gin and tonics flowing, we chatter away and Bobbie saunters in, glowering at our guests. Every so often, she'll allow one of us to give her a quick stroke, then she retreats to the bedroom. I envy her, because after a few drinks, I'm sleepy, and despite a lovely few hours, I'm glad when we say our goodbyes and I can hit the hay. I must be getting old.

Under 20 minutes | Makes one large bowl

Ingredients

For the salad
− Half a large celeriac (around 200g), peeled and grated
− 1 x 400g can cannellini beans
        (chickpeas or butter beans will also work well),
        rinsed and drained
− 4 tbsp extra virgin olive oil
− 1 tbsp apple cider vinegar
− 1–2 cloves garlic, peeled
− The juice of 1 lemon
− 1 tbsp tahini
− 1 tsp dried thyme
− Salt and pepper

Simply put all the ingredients into a bowl and blend using a hand-held blender – or pop them into a food processor or blender and blitz. Serve with a drizzle of olive oil and a sprinkling of thyme.

Roasted Jerusalem artichokes

December tends to be a quiet month workwise, but so far it's been relentlessly busy with several deadlines vying for my attention. It's the week before Christmas and I take a walk to clear my head. Around the lake, I see a couple feeding a tiny robin and I stop to watch. This simple act, an innocent creature in the wild, brings me back to earth.

When I get home, I roast some Jerusalem artichokes for dinner. These knobbly brown roots might not look very jolly, but they're sweetly mellow and full of vitamin C, potassium and iron. I dress these as I would potatoes, with lots of oil and lemon juice, and they're a revelation: luxuriously tender and zesty. I decide to make them more often.

45 minutes | Serves 2-3

Ingredients

– 500g Jerusalem artichokes
– 3 tbsp vegetable, olive or rapeseed oil
– The juice of 1 lemon
– Salt and pepper

Preheat the oven to 200C. Pour the oil into a large ovenproof dish and put into the oven for 5 minutes. Scrub or peel the artichokes and cut into half. Remove the dish from the oven and add the artichokes, then pour over the lemon juice and season with salt and pepper. Place on the middle shelf of the oven and roast for 30 minutes.

Jewelled red cabbage

Today is the winter solstice and after this it's only a matter of time until, day by day, slowly but surely, it will get lighter and brighter. This morning, holding a mug of coffee, I walk out onto the street and watch the sun rise. Amidst the Christmas chaos, it's a rare moment of peace.

On this dark and now drizzly day, I want cheer, and set about making a festive side dish, which we'll eat on Christmas Eve – and perhaps on the big day itself, too. Braised red cabbage takes a little while to cook, but it's worth the wait, and soon the entire flat smells like mulled wine. When it's served, I'll scatter over pomegranate seeds, glistening red rubies which add a juicy crunch. It's beginning to look a lot like Christmas.

1 hour 45 minutes | Serves 6

Ingredients

- 1 large red cabbage
- 100g soft light brown sugar
- 75ml cider vinegar
- 200ml red wine
- The juice of 2 oranges
- 1 cinnamon stick
- Salt and pepper
- A grating of fresh nutmeg
- 1 pomegranate

Quarter the red cabbage and remove the core, then finely shred. Tip into a large pan with brown sugar, cider vinegar, red wine, orange juice and the cinnamon stick and season well, then grate over the nutmeg. Bring to a simmer, then cover with a lid, lower the heat and cook for 1.5 hours, stirring every so often. Remove the cinnamon stick, then cut the pomegranate in half, bash to remove the seeds and scatter over the red cabbage.

This will keep for a few days, or can be frozen for two months. Reheat until piping hot.

Parsnip, pecan and polenta loaf

C hristmas Eve. I like the light this morning with the sun low in the sky. With presents still unwrapped and family to visit, I wander through the woods seeking stillness. Tonight, I'll make a festive loaf for tomorrow's lunch, or in all likelihood, dinner. We've always eaten late on Christmas Day, taking our time to open presents and enjoy a couple of drinks. Tomorrow, we'll take a morning stroll, so I need something ready to pop in the oven while I make the side dishes.

This loaf is rich and moist – much tastier than turkey in my opinion – and it really sings for its supper. I make this listening to Carols from Kings, a tradition as familiar to me as Santa and stockings. This is Christmas.

1 hour 30 minutes, plus cooling time | Serves 3-4

Ingredients

- 2 tbsp rapeseed oil
- 1 small carrot, peeled and diced
- 3 shallots, peeled and diced
- 2 cloves garlic, peeled and crushed
- 4-5 fresh sage leaves, snipped with
    scissors (or use 1 tsp dried sage)
- 1 x 400g can chickpeas,
    rinsed and drained
- 3-4 large parsnips (around 300g),
    peeled and grated

- 100g quick-cook polenta
- 1 tsp ground allspice
- 1 tbsp apple cider
    or balsamic vinegar
- 2 tbsp olive oil
- 2 tbsp maple syrup
- The juice of 1 orange
- 150g pecans
- 50ml oat milk
- Salt and pepper)

Preheat the oven to 180C. Grease a 9×5 inch loaf tin, and then line it with a piece of greaseproof paper cut to fit the length of the pan. In a large pan, fry the shallots, garlic, sage and carrot in the oil over a medium heat for 5-6 minutes.

Tip the chickpeas into a large bowl and roughly mash. Add the grated parsnip and all the other ingredients (apart from the pecans), plus the fried shallot mixture and stir well. If the mixture seems dry, add a little more oat milk or water and mix again. Take half the pecans and roughly break into pieces, then tip into the mixture and stir well. Press all of the loaf mixture into the prepared loaf tin. Pack it down as firmly as you can as this will help it hold together after cooling.

Bake the loaf uncovered for 45-50 minutes until the edges start to darken and the loaf is semi-firm to the touch. Place the loaf tin directly onto a cooling rack for 15 minutes. Then, slide a knife around the ends to loosen, and carefully lift out the loaf tin (using the greaseproof paper as 'handles') and place it directly onto the cooling rack for another 30 minutes. Decorate the top of the loaf with the rest of the pecans.

After cooling, carefully slice the loaf into slabs and serve. Drizzle over a little extra maple syrup when serving, if you like.

Stir-fried sprouts
with orange and cashews

On Boxing Day, we go for a walk. It's good to stretch the legs. I like the period between Christmas and the New Year (some call it Twixmas), but I'm feeling a bit stir crazy with all the eating, drinking and lolling around. Tomorrow I'll go to the gym and plan the year ahead so that starting work again next week isn't too painful.

The fridge is groaning with leftovers and I know for certain that there are some sprouts lurking in the salad drawer. I want a fresh and vibrant dish so I make this simple stir-fry.

Under 15 minutes | Serves 2

Ingredients

For the stir-fry
− 2 tbsp sesame oil
− 100g sprouts with the ends removed and finely sliced
− 3 big handfuls of kale, spinach or other greens
− 50g cashews
− 2 tsp sesame seeds

For the dressing
− 1 orange, juice and zest
− 2 tbsp soy sauce
− 1 tbsp sesame oil
− 1 inch ginger, peeled and grated
− 1 chilli, deseeded and finely sliced

Heat the oil in a large frying pan or wok. Add the sprouts and kale and the nuts and cook for another 5-6 minutes or so. In a bowl, mix the orange juice and zest with the soy sauce, the chilli and the ginger and in the last minute of cooking, pour over the stir-fry and stir. You can also add some of the orange flesh, if you like. When cooked, sprinkle with sesame seeds and serve.

Celery soup

After taking down the Christmas tree down last night, it's time to dust off the cobwebs. I go to the library, which in Swansea is brutalist and beautiful and overlooks the beach. Even though it's grey outside, I've had worse views, although I'd be happier if people wouldn't talk – it is a library, after all.

I arrive home, after a blustery walk, craving something warm and soothing on this joyless January day. I make celery soup and think of my mum. One day, before I was born, my mum was making celery soup. She put it in the blender, pressed the button, but had forgotten to put the lid on. Whoosh! Green soup went everywhere. A man walking past the house was horrified to see soup splatter against the window. It's a cautionary tale, and as a result, I've always been careful with kitchen gadgets.

40 minutes | Serves 3-4

Ingredients

– 1 tbsp olive oil
– 1 large onion or two shallots, peeled and diced
– 2 cloves garlic, peeled and crushed
– 8 stalks celery, ends removed and diced
– 1 tsp celery salt
– ½ tsp sea salt
– Freshly ground pepper
– 500ml hot vegetable stock

In a large pan, heat the oil over a medium temperature and fry the onion and garlic for 3 minutes. Add the celery, the celery salt and the salt and pepper and fry for 5 minutes. Pour over the vegetable stock and bring to the boil, then reduce the heat, cover with a lid and simmer for 20 minutes. Once cooked, blitz with a hand-held blender and serve with crusty bread.

Spaghetti carbonara with a creamy cauliflower sauce

The winter months are always hard, especially once the fun and fizz of Christmas is over but as every day inches closer to brighter skies, I feel hopeful. I'm struggling with the dark, dark nights and the particularly grey days so I eke out as much sunlight as I can.

Today there are beautiful blue skies in Swansea, but it's cold. It's early January, but work shows no sign of slowing down. It's been a busy week and a night on the sofa is calling, so I make my version of a comforting classic: spaghetti carbonara. Cauliflower and sprouts are cheap and plentiful at this time of year, and blended with oat milk, they make a silky sauce for spaghetti. If you can't find nutritional yeast, you can use a few tablespoons of soy sauce or a little Marmite instead.

Under 25 minutes | Serves 2

Ingredients

– 1 small cauliflower (around 300g),
     broken into small florets
– 200g sprouts, outer leaves and stalks
     removed and cut into half
– 100g mushrooms, roughly sliced
– 2 shallots, peeled and finely chopped
– 1 clove garlic, peeled and finely chopped
– 1 tbsp olive oil
– 400ml oat milk
– The juice of half a lemon
– 3-4 tbsp nutritional yeast
– 1 tsp miso paste
– A liberal grating of nutmeg
– Salt and pepper
– 150g spaghetti

Bring a large pan of water to the boil, then add the cauliflower florets and sprouts and boil for 7–8 minutes. Drain and set aside to cool.

Meanwhile, over a medium heat, fry the shallots and mushrooms in the oil for 5 minutes, then add the garlic and fry for another 2 minutes. Set aside.

Bring another large pan (if you want to save on washing up, use the same one as before) to the boil and add a pinch of salt. Cook the spaghetti for 8–10 minutes.

While the spaghetti is cooking, put the cauliflower and sprouts in a food processor with half the oat milk and pulse until smooth. Pour the mixture into a pan and add the rest of the oat milk, the nutritional yeast, lemon juice, miso paste and a grating of nutmeg. Stir together and heat on a low heat for 2–3 minutes, stirring frequently.

Drain the spaghetti (keeping a little of the pasta water) and return to the pan. Pour over the carbonara sauce, then stir in the mushrooms and shallots and a little bit of pasta water. Stir together and serve.

Pearl barley, butterbean and cauliflower stew

I've eaten for Wales since Christmas and I'm not planning to stop any time soon. It's a dreary day, rainy and cold outside, but as I'm having a quiet weekend, I'm not too bothered.

I don't always have time to cook, especially when I'm working to a deadline, so at the weekends, if I can be bothered, I batch cook. I make a warm and comforting stew that should provide a couple of meals during the week and stop me from snacking on toast all day when I'm up against it. Good old cauliflower makes yet another appearance in this one-pot meal, and miso paste adds depth, but you can use 2-3 tablespoons of soy sauce instead.

Under 15 minutes | Serves 3-4

Ingredients

— 1 small cauliflower, broken into florets
— 1 onion, peeled and diced
— 1 clove of garlic, peeled and finely chopped
— 1 tsp caraway seeds
— 2 bay leaves
— 1-2 tbsp rapeseed oil
— 2 tsp miso paste
— 1 x 400g can of tomatoes, chopped or plum
— 1 x 400g can of butterbeans, drained
— 2 carrots, peeled and roughly chopped
— 150g pearl barley
— 150g fresh or frozen spinach
— Salt and pepper

Heat the oil over a medium heat in a large pan or heat-proof casserole dish, then fry the onion and garlic for 2-3 minutes. Add the carrot and cauliflower and fry for another 3 minutes, then tip in the tomatoes (fill the empty can with water and add that too) and the pearl barley, caraway seeds, bay leaves and miso paste. Season with salt and pepper.

Bring to the boil, then reduce the heat, add a lid to the pan and cook for 15 minutes. Add the spinach and butterbeans and cook for another 10-15 (again, with the lid on).

Remove the bay leaves and serve with bread or green vegetables.

Lazy mushroom and lentil pie

Working on a Sunday's not so bad, especially as I'm proofreading some short stories which are rather good. I've just paid my first tax return, a not altogether pleasant experience as anyone who's self-employed can testify, but I feel pleased, almost proud of myself. Freelancing is tough at times, but I'm glad that I've made a go of it.

It's raining outside, and miserable weather calls for pie. I make what I call a lazy pie using ready-made pastry because I can't be bothered to make my own. Because I have just the one sheet, I use it to top the pie filling, and it's a lighter, but still lovely, dinner as a result. Once in the oven, the pie is ready in half an hour, which gives me enough time to make some mashed potato and boil some vegetables. Voila: easy comfort food.

Under 1 hour

Ingredients

– 2 tbsp rapeseed oil
– 500g mushrooms, sliced
– 2 cloves garlic, peeled and crushed
– The juice of 1 lemon
– 5-6 fresh sage leaves, cut finely (or use 1 tsp dried sage)
– Salt and pepper
– 1 x 400g can brown or green lentils, rinsed and drained
– 1 heaped tsp wholegrain mustard
– 1 tsp vegetable stock powder
– 150ml oat milk, plus a little extra for brushing the pastry
– 1 x 375g puff pastry sheet

Preheat the oven to 200C. In a large pan, heat the oil over a medium temperature. Add the mushrooms, garlic, half the lemon juice and the sage leaves and season with salt and pepper. Fry for 6-7 minutes or until golden. Add the lentils and the rest of the lemon juice and fry for a further 2 minutes. Add the mustard, stock powder and oat milk, reduce the heat and cook for another 5 minutes. Take a large rectangular ovenproof dish and evenly spread the pie filling across the base. Cover with the pastry sheet and press down gently. Trim or fold down any excess pastry, then brush the whole of the sheet with oat milk. Place the dish on the middle shelf of the oven and bake for 30-35 minutes.

Beetroot and hazelnut soup

I'm feeling a bit out of sorts this week. The dark days are getting to me and I'm tired and unmotivated. In an attempt to claw back some cheer, I make a bright beetroot and hazelnut soup.

It's the little things that make me happy. As a freelancer, it's being able to work from home under a blanket, with a cat sleeping at my feet while I tap away at my laptop. It's when Kieron brings me a cup of coffee in bed when he gets up before me. It's this vibrant soup. I make a list of these things and make a note to look at it when I'm next feeling blue.

Under 40 minutes | Serves 3-4

Ingredients

- 1 large onion, peeled and diced
- 2 garlic cloves, peeled and crushed
- 5-6 beetroot (600-700g), including tops,
    peeled or scrubbed and roughly diced
- 1 tbsp oil
- 750ml hot vegetable stock
- 2 tsp carraway seeds
- 100g hazelnuts, plus extra for garnishing
- 150ml oat milk
- 1 tsp sumac
- 1 tsp chilli flakes
- Salt and pepper

In a large pan, heat the oil over a low heat. Fry the onions and garlic for 2-3 minutes. Add the beetroot (set aside the tops and leaves for later) and the carraway seeds and cook for 10 minutes. Add the hot stock and bring to the boil, then reduce the heat, add the beetroot tops and cover with a lid. Simmer for 15 minutes, then add the hazelnuts and the oat milk. Cook for another 5 minutes, then turn off the heat and add the sumac and chilli flakes and a little salt and pepper. Using a hand-held blender or a food processor, blitz until smooth. Serve with extra hazelnuts and a little extra virgin olive oil and a dollop of vegan yogurt or crème fraîche, if you like.

Keralan cauliflower and pineapple curry

Today's a quiet day. I meet a friend for coffee (which, even after two years of free-lancing, makes me feel a bit like I'm playing truant from work) and go to the gym. After that, I retreat to the sofa, do some writing and drink mug after mug of tea.

I'm very hungry after the gym so tonight I'll make curry for dinner. It's another dull afternoon and I think back to sunnier days, and one in particular at Hay Festival where I enjoyed a delicious Keralan cauliflower and pineapple curry. I have cauliflower in the fridge so I head to the supermarket to pick up a pineapple (imported pineapples are at their best in January and February), and make my own version of this fruity, fragrant dish.

Under 40 minutes | Serves 3-4

Ingredients

- 1 tsp coconut oil
- 1 large cauliflower, cut into florets and leaves reserved
- 3-4 curry leaves
- 1 x 400ml can full-fat coconut milk
- 1 x 400g can chickpeas, rinsed and drained
- 200g spinach
- 1 medium pineapple, peeled and cut into small chunks
- 1 lime (juice only)
- 75g cashews

For the curry paste

- 1 small onion, peeled and diced
- 2 inches fresh ginger, peeled
- 1 red chilli, deseeded and roughly sliced
- 1 clove garlic, peeled
- 1 lime (juice)
- 1 tsp mustard seeds
- 1 tsp ground cinnamon
- 1 tsp ground turmeric
- 1 tsp ground fenugreek
- 1 tsp coriander seeds
- 1 tbsp brown sugar
- A pinch of sea salt
- A little water

In a large pan, heat the coconut oil over a medium heat. Fry the cauliflower florets and leaves with the curry leaves for 10-15 minutes.

Meanwhile, place all the curry paste ingredients into a bowl and blitz using a hand-held blender (alternatively, you can blitz them in a food processor).

Add the coconut milk and curry paste to the pan and bring to the boil. Reduce the heat and add the chickpeas. Simmer for 5 minutes then add the spinach and pineapple. Cook for another 2-3 minutes, then turn off the heat and stir through the cashews and the lime juice. Serve with rice.

French onion soup

It might be a short and dark month, but I like February, although perhaps only because it's when my birthday falls. This year, we spend the weekend in Bath. It's been snowing everywhere except Swansea, but once we drive over the mint green Severn Bridge, the sky an electric blue, everything is white. When we arrive in Bath, it's blanketed in thick snow and there is a strange and soundless stillness to the usually bustling city centre.

We eat at Acorn where the food is exquisite, and the next evening, happy but hungover, I make French onion soup, stinking out the flat in the process. It's worth it though because a bowl of this is like a big cwtch – just what's needed in this chilly weather. I add Marmite for a rich and meaty flavour and slurp away to my heart's content.

1 hour 30 minutes | Serves 3-4

Ingredients

– 2 tbsp olive oil
– 50g vegan butter
– 1 tbsp brown sugar
– 5 onions (about 700g), peeled and thinly sliced
– 2 cloves garlic, peeled and crushed
– 1 litre vegetable stock
– 2 tbsp Marmite
– 2 tbsp plain flour

Place a large pan or casserole on a high heat and melt the oil and butter together. Add the onions, garlic and sugar, and sweat for 5-6 minutes, stirring occasionally. Reduce the heat to its lowest setting, place a lid on the pan and leave the onions to carry on cooking very slowly for about 30 minutes, by which time the base of the pan will be covered with a rich, nut brown, caramelised film. Pour in the stock and add the Marmite and the flour, season, then stir with a wooden spoon, scraping the base of the pan well.

Bring to the boil, then reduce the heat and simmer without a lid for another 30 minutes. Ladle into bowls and serve with crusty bread.

Slow roasted beets with radicchio, chickpeas and hazelnuts

I n the early hours of the morning, I'm woken by the wind howling angrily. It's door and window rattlingly furious. I'm a light sleeper so I lie awake as Kieron slumbers, and eventually I get up to make some coffee and read.

I'm at home today, so feeling sleepy, I potter about, half-heartedly planning the next few weeks and doing some housework. I go for a long walk in an effort to feel more awake, then spend the afternoon lounging on the sofa with Bobbie. I need a bath and an early night, but first a soothing supper of roasted beets and radicchio, which is light but sustaining and sees me through the next few hours until I climb into bed.

1 hour 45 minutes | Serves 2

Ingredients

- 4-5 beetroot, skin on
- 1 tbsp white wine vinegar
- 1 tbsp soy sauce
- 1 tbsp sesame oil
- 1 tbsp maple syrup
- 1 x 400g can chickpeas, rinsed and drained
- 1 head radicchio
- 25g hazelnut, roughly chopped

Preheat the oven to 200C. Mix together the white wine vinegar, soy sauce, sesame oil and maple syrup, the put the beetroot in an oven dish and pour over the dressing. Roast for an hour and a half, adding a little water to the dish at intervals so that you make a nice little juice. Relax, do the dishes or whatever you fancy. When cooked, put the beets aside and marinate the chickpeas in the beetroot juice for 10-15 minutes. Shred the radicchio and divide onto two plates or bowls. Chop the beets in half, spoon over the chickpeas and pour over the rest of the sauce. Sprinkle over the hazelnuts and enjoy.

Kohlrabi, celeriac and apple casserole

Monday mornings aren't enjoyed by many of us, but once in a while, I quite like the first day of the working week. Gone is last week's negative Nancy and in her place is a shiny new me with a can-do attitude. This glow lasts until my morning coffee – always two mugs – has worn off.

I'm feeling bright because Bobbie, after an emergency trip to the vet over the weekend, is better. Tonight, we have some quality time together as 'Dad' is at band practice, and we settle down on the sofa – she's not allowed outside for a little while. I make a stew with kohlrabi, which is always a treat to find at the greengrocer. It's no looker but has a mild and slightly sweet taste, which is just the comforter I need.

Under 40 minutes | Serves 3-4

Ingredients

– 1 tbsp sesame oil
– 1 shallot, peeled and diced
– 1 large garlic clove, peeled and crushed
– 1 kohlrabi (200g), peeled and diced
– Half a celeriac (200g), peeled and diced
– 1 apple, cored and diced
– 2 tbsp soy sauce
– 1 x 400g can tomatoes
– 1 tsp miso paste
– 1 heaped tbsp peanut butter
– 1 x 400g can chickpeas, rinsed and drained
– The juice of 1 lime
– Parsley/coriander

Heat the sesame oil over a medium temperature in a large pan and fry the shallot and garlic for 2-3 minutes. Add the kohlrabi, celeriac and apple and fry for 5 minutes. Add the tomatoes (half fill the empty can with water and add this to the pan) with the miso paste and peanut butter and bring to the boil. Lower the heat, cover with a lid and simmer for 15 minutes. Add the chickpeas, turn up the heat and cook for another 5 minutes. Turn off the heat, stir through the lime juice and serve with some parsley/coriander.

Chocolate and beetroot brownies

The weather today is utterly miserable. I'm still in my pyjamas, eating a late breakfast and feeling a bit sorry for myself. I'm more owl than lark and I can be quite maudlin in the mornings. There is light at the end of the tunnel though, because in just a few weeks, the clocks go forward and British Summertime begins.

It's a day for baking, and after an hour or so of writing – or trying to, at least, for I've hit a block – I turn on the oven and make some chocolate brownies. I add beetroot for a rich and earthy flavour, and I'm pleased with how moreish they are. I retreat to my makeshift desk on the sofa with a slice and a cup of tea and get back to work.

1 hour 40 minutes | Makes 12 brownies

Ingredients

- 250g beetroot, peeled and cut into cubes
- 200g plain flour
- 1 tsp baking powder
- 1 tsp bicarbonate of soda
- 3 tbsp cocoa powder
- 1 tsp ground cinnamon

- 150g vegan butter or margarine (at room temperature)
- 150g brown sugar
- 50ml plant milk
- 100g dark chocolate, broken into chunks (or chocolate chips)
- 1 tsp vanilla extract
- A pinch of sea salt (optional)

Preheat the oven to 200C and line an 8-inch brownie tin with greaseproof paper.

Prepare the beetroot and place in a dish with 2-3 tbsp water. Place on the top shelf of the oven and roast for an hour.

Meanwhile, make your brownie batter by sieving the flour, baking powder, bicarbonate of soda, cocoa powder and cinnamon into a large bowl and mixing together. In another large bowl, beat the butter, sugar, milk and vanilla extract. Slowly beat in the flour mixture.

Remove the beetroot from the oven and reduce the temperature to 180C. Set aside the beetroot and allow to cool, then blend into a purée using a hand-held mixer or a food processor.

Stir the beetroot purée and chocolate pieces into the cake mixture until you have a thick batter. Add a generous pinch of salt, if you like. Pour the batter into the lined tin and spread evenly. Bake for 25-30 minutes – you'll know if they're cooked if a baking skewer inserted into the cake comes out clean. Place on a cooling rack and allow to cool completely (if you don't you'll have very tasty, but very crumbly brownies) before slicing into 12 pieces. These should keep in an airtight container for 2–3 days.

Quinoa and brown rice salad with purple sprouting broccoli and blood orange

It might still be February, but I can smell spring in the air today. I'm in Cardiff to have coffee with a new work client and afterwards I meet a friend for lunch. We catch up over pizza and fizzy pop upstairs at Cardiff Market, watching the hustle and bustle below.

When I get home I'm in a sunny mood, as I often am after a good chat, and the longer and lighter days are helping too. I make a colourful and crunchy salad with blood orange and purple sprouting broccoli – I want to make the most of these late winter wonders while I can – and a bright and punchy dressing.

Under 30 minutes | Serves 2

Ingredients

– 75g brown rice, rinsed and drained
– 75g quinoa, rinsed and drained
– 8-10 stems of purple sprouting broccoli (about 125g)
– 1 and a half blood oranges
– 2 large handfuls of spinach
– A handful of fresh dill
– 25g whole almonds (optional)
– 1 tbsp rapeseed oil
– Salt and pepper

For the dressing

– 2 tbsp extra virgin olive oil
– The juice of half a blood orange
– The juice of half a lime
– Salt and pepper

Bring a pan of salted water to the boil, then reduce the heat and cook the rice for 15 minutes, and add the quinoa to the same pan and cook for another 10 minutes. Drain and set aside. Meanwhile, heat a large heavy based pan over a medium heat and add the rapeseed oil. Fry the broccoli for 3-4 minutes, turning occasionally, then add the almonds and fry for another 2-3 minutes. Turn off the heat.

Take a large serving dish and add the spinach leaves. Make the dressing by mixing all the ingredients, then spoon half of it over the spinach and massage. Add the rice and quinoa to the serving dish and pour over the rest of the dressing. Add the broccoli and the almonds, then peel and segment one of the oranges Add these to the salad, then roughly chop the dill and add that to the bowl. Take the remaining orange half and squeeze over the salad, then season with salt and pepper and serve.

Root vegetable shepherd's pie

What to do on a rainy Sunday evening? I have the flat myself, Bobbie is asleep on my lap, and I'm reading a good book.

I make a big shepherd's pie with carrots, parsnips, turnips, swede and celeriac and it's good, really good, even if it does take some time to assemble and cook. I eat mine as I always do: with peas, a slice of white bread and butter and a dollop of HP sauce. I serve myself a generous portion, but barely make a dent in the dish, so I'll have plenty for leftovers during the week. After washing up, I decide to go to bed with my book – and Bobbie. After all, an early night is the best start to the week ahead.

1 hour 45 minutes | Serves 6-8

Ingredients

– 1kg potatoes, peeled or scrubbed and cut into small chunks
– 2 tbsp olive oil
– 1 onion, peeled and diced
– 1 clove garlic, peeled and crushed
– 150g mushrooms, sliced
– 1 tsp fresh thyme leaves (or 1 tsp dried thyme)
– 1 large carrot, peeled and diced
– 1 large parsnip, peeled and diced
– Half a celeriac, peeled and diced
– Half a swede, peeled and diced
– 1 large turnip, peeled and diced
– 200g green lentils, rinsed and drained
– 3 tbsp tomato purée
– A few dashes of vegan Worcestershire sauce
– 1 tbsp Marmite or yeast extract
– 500ml hot vegetable stock
– 100ml vegan red wine (or 100ml hot vegetable stock)
– A grating of fresh nutmeg (or ½ tsp nutmeg powder)
– Salt and pepper
– 50g vegan butter or margarine
– 100ml oat milk

Bring a large pan of salted water to the boil, then boil the potatoes for about 30 minutes or until soft. Once boiled, turn off the heat and leave in the cooking water.

In a large pan, heat the oil over a medium temperature and fry the onion and garlic for 2-3 minutes, then add the mushrooms and the thyme and fry for another 3 minutes. Add the root vegetables and fry for 3 minutes, then add the lentils, Marmite, Worcestershire sauce, nutmeg and tomato purée and pour over the stock. Bring to the boil, then reduce the heat, cover with a lid and simmer for 30-35 minutes, stirring occasionally. In the last 10 minutes, add the wine or extra stock and stir through.

Preheat the oven to 200C. Take a large ovenproof dish and spread the lentil sauce across the base of the dish, making sure that it's even. Drain the potatoes, then return to the pan and add the oat milk, butter and salt and pepper and mash. Layer evenly over the lentil layer and add a little more grated nutmeg, if you like. Place on the top shelf of the oven and cook for 20 minutes and serve.

Swede gratin with miso and maple syrup

The days might be getting longer but it's still coat and gloves weather – for me, anyway. In our house, I'm the only one who feels the cold, while Kieron often goes out without a jacket. So yes, we've argued about the central heating.

The course of true love never did run smooth, but he's a good egg, really: he's loyal and patient and helps me see the funny side of things, so I can't complain. I'm very hungry tonight so for dinner I make a swede gratin, adding miso and maple syrup, and it's so delicious that I have to stop myself from eating the entire thing.

1 hour 45 minutes | Serves 4-6

Ingredients

- 2 large swedes, peeled and sliced thinly, lengthways
- 2 tbsp rapeseed oil
- 2 garlic cloves, peeled and crushed
- 3 tbsp plain flour
- A generous pinch of salt
- 500ml oat milk
- 250ml vegetable stock
- 1 tbsp apple cider vinegar
- 2 heaped tsp white miso paste
- 2 tbsp maple syrup
- Salt and pepper
- A grating of fresh nutmeg

First of all, make the sauce. Heat the oil in a large saucepan over a medium heat, then add the garlic and sauté for 2-3 minutes, until soft and translucent. Add the flour and salt and stir rapidly. Cook for a minute, then gradually add the plant milk and hot stock and stir through, then add the miso paste, maple syrup and vinegar. Cook for another 5 minutes, stirring all the while. Try to get out all the lumps if you can.

Now, turn the oven on to 200C. Slice the swede thinly, then use a little oil to grease a casserole or large ovenproof dish. Spread a layer of slices along the bottom and cover with some of the sauce. Add another layer of swede and add more sauce, then place a final layer of swede on top and season with salt and pepper and a grating of fresh nutmeg. Cover with a lid or foil and place on the top shelf of the oven. Bake for 45 minutes then remove the lid or foil and bake for another 25-30 minutes, until golden brown. For a really crisp topping, place it under the grill (lid off) for the final 5 minutes.

Thank yous

Thank you for buying this book. It means a lot to share my recipes with you and I hope that you enjoy them. Writing *The Seasonal Vegan* was no mean feat, and very challenging at times, so I'm grateful to those who supported me throughout the process.

Thank you to the incredibly talented Manon for making my food look so beautiful and for being a great working partner and friend. Thank you to everyone at Seren. Thank you to Alison, Becky, Caitlin, Danielle, Debra, Ellie, Rachel and Jon, Rhodd, Rosie and Dean, Sareta, and Yvonne and Graham for testing the recipes and providing such helpful feedback

Thank you to Tom at Blaencamel Farm for supplying fruit and vegetables for many of the photos and for all your expert knowledge which proved extremely useful.

Thank you to my friends and family. Finally, thank you to Kieron, Seren and Bobbie the cat for all the love and laughter.

Index

Notes

Notes